SPECIAL PRAISE FOR *ROOTS AND WINGS*

"*Roots and Wings* is one of those rare, beautiful books that will teach and touch you. Exploring the difficult and meaningful work of parenting, it brings together so many insightful and useful ideas from solid research and psychological theory in the areas of attachment, human development, mindfulness, addiction, and recovery. With his down-to-earth style and wry wit, Dan Mager poignantly reflects on his own parenting journey and invites us all to join him in facing ourselves in order to do and be better."

Jennifer Kunst, PhD
Clinical psychologist and psychoanalyst
and author of *Wisdom from the Couch*

* * *

"*Roots and Wings* is one of the best books on parenting I've read. This is remarkable because it's technically a book about parenting while in recovery from addiction. Based on personal experience, Dan Mager describes how the self-knowledge and skills gained through recovery can dramatically improve your parenting skills *and* how being a parent can be a tremendous aid to recovery. I love how practical the book is. In it, you'll find a broad range of helpful tools—from easy-to-learn mindfulness practices, to the invaluable parenting skill of "active listening," to learning to understand your child at different stages of their development. Don't pass up this gem of a book. It gets my highest recommendation."

Toni Bernhard
Author of *How to Wake Up, How to Be Sick,* and
How to Live Well with Chronic Pain and Illness

"*Roots and Wings* is truly a precious gift to all parents in recovery. Dan Mager skillfully unlocks the wisdom teachings of recovery and mindfulness to provide readers with authentic, practical, and accessible tools to create a healthy, healing, and nurturing environment for parents and their children to flourish."

John Bruna
Mindfulness and dharma teacher, cofounder of the Mindful
Life Program, and author of *The Wisdom of a Meaningful Life*

* * *

"This is a powerful book that every parent needs to read! Deep understanding and compassion for the complexities of parenting permeate Dan Mager's comprehensive approach on how to integrate mindfulness into the raising of a child. *Roots and Wings* is both incredibly practical and spiritual at the same time."

Claudia Black, PhD
Clinical architect of the Claudia Black Young Adult Center at The
Meadows and author of *It Will Never Happen to Me* and *Unspoken Legacy*

* * *

"Dan Mager has a rare ability to articulate the deep insights gained from extensive personal experience in twelve-step recovery and the practice of mindfulness in ways that readers can begin to apply immediately. *Roots and Wings* offers a wealth of stories and strategies grounded in the art of healing, growing our capacity for love and skillfulness in interpersonal relationships, and transforming unhealthful habit energies in ourselves and our loved ones. While this wonderful book is framed for mindful parenting, it is a tremendous resource for anyone in recovery or on any path of spiritual awakening."

Peter Kuhn
Buddhist priest ordained by Thich Nhat Hanh, twelve-step Buddhist
workshop and retreat facilitator, writer, and jazz musician

"*Roots and Wings* is a unique volume that addresses the challenges of parenting for people in recovery from addiction. Dan Mager brings together mindfulness practices, twelve-step-oriented recovery, and neuroscience, with psychological/developmental theory and aspects of contemporary counseling approaches in ways that can help parents dramatically increase their awareness and skills. This book is rich with information and guidance that will be incredibly valuable to all parents—not just those in recovery."

Mel Pohl, MD, DFASAM
Chief Medical Officer, Las Vegas Recovery Center, and author
of *A Day without Pain, Pain Recovery,* and *The Pain Antidote*

* * *

"As a person in long-term recovery, I have both experienced and witnessed my share of unskillful parenting. *Roots and Wings* responds to a deep need within the culture of recovery and is long overdue. Dan Mager presents the obstacles with great clarity and proceeds to lay out effective yet simple changes that parents can institute immediately and continue to build upon with a foundation of mindfulness practice. I cannot wait to refer this book to others."

Gregory S. Pergament
Ordained Zen Buddhist and Taoist priest
and author of *Chi Kung in Recovery*

ROOTS AND WINGS

DAN MAGER

ROOTS AND *Wings*

MINDFUL PARENTING
IN RECOVERY

CRP
CENTRAL RECOVERY PRESS
LAS VEGAS

Central Recovery Press (CRP) is committed to publishing exceptional materials addressing addiction treatment, recovery, and behavioral healthcare topics.

For more information, visit www.centralrecoverypress.com.

Publisher: Central Recovery Press
3321 N. Buffalo Drive
Las Vegas, NV 89129

23 22 21 20 19 18   1 2 3 4 5

Library of Congress Cataloging-in-Publication Data

Names: Mager, Dan, author.
Title: Roots and wings : mindful parenting in recovery / Dan Mager.
Description: Las Vegas, NV : Central Recovery Press, [2018]
Identifiers: LCCN 2017059338 (print) | LCCN 2018001945 (ebook) | ISBN 9781942094685 (ebook) | ISBN 9781942094678 (pbk. : alk. paper)
Subjects: LCSH: Recovering alcoholics--Family relationships. | Parenting. | Mindfulness (Psychology) | Children of alcoholics.
Classification: LCC HV5132 (ebook) | LCC HV5132 .M337 2018 (print) | DDC 649/.10874--dc23
LC record available at https://lccn.loc.gov/2017059338

Photo of Dan Mager by Central Recovery Press. Used with permission.

The Twelve Steps of Narcotics Anonymous reprinted by permission of NA World Services, Inc. All rights reserved. The Twelve Steps of NA reprinted for adaptation by permission of AA World Services, Inc.

"Brokedown Palace," Words by Robert Hunter Music by Jerry Garcia.
Copyright © 1971, Ice Nine Publishing Co., Inc. Copyright renewed.
All rights administered by Universal Music Corporation
All rights reserved. Used by permission. Reprinted by permission of Hal Leonard, LLC.

Lyrics from *Brokedown Palace* by Robert Hunter/Jerry Garcia used with permission.

Every attempt has been made to contact copyright holders. If copyright holders have not been properly acknowledged please contact us. Central Recovery Press will be happy to rectify the omission in future printings of this book.

Publisher's Note:
This book contains general information about addiction recovery, parenting, and mindfulness. The information is not medical advice. This book is not an alternative to medical advice from your doctor or other professional healthcare provider.

Our books represent the experiences and opinions of their authors only. Every effort has been made to ensure that events, institutions, and statistics presented in our books as facts are accurate and up-to-date. To protect their privacy, the names of some of the people, places, and institutions in this book may have been changed.

Cover and interior design by Sara Streifel, Think Creative Design

Dedicated to

My father, Art,
the personification of dedication
and perseverance,
who could be hard as granite,
but gave me both grace and mercy.

My mother, Sandy,
the embodiment of persistence
and patience,
who showed me the possibilities
of elegance in adaptation.

My daughters,
who hold my heart,
and continue to gift me with
exquisite and ongoing opportunities
to practice what I preach.

TABLE OF CONTENTS

Acknowledgments xiii

Introduction xv

CHAPTER ONE
Recovery, Parenting, and Mindfulness, Oh My 1

    Reframing Karma 3

    Suiting up and Showing up 4

    Actualizing the Serenity Prayer 5

    Parenting as Service 8

    A Quality Holding Environment 9

    Hugs Not Drugs 10

    A Brief Introduction to Mindfulness 11

    Trail Finding and Following 12

    Perfection Is Bullshit 13

    Putting the Pieces Together 14

CHAPTER TWO
Roots Then Wings 17

    Familiarity through Transition 18

Strengthening Roots through Protection
and Family Rituals 20

Life Is a Developmental Process 23

Erikson's Stages of Psychosocial Development 24

Change Is the Only Constant 31

When Helping Hinders 33

CHAPTER THREE
Growing Beyond How You Grew up 37

A Different Kind of Attachment 39

Trauma Is More Common than You Think 43

The Effects of Trauma 44

Trauma Takes Many Forms 45

Small-t Traumas 46

The Relationship between Trauma and Addiction 47

Healing from Trauma 48

Change Is a Motherf'er 51

The Transtheoretical Model of Change 51

Principles of Behavior Change 53

Awareness and Action 53

The Four Stages of Learning and Skill Development 54

Experience Changes the Brain 56

Expanding Feelings of Kindness, Appreciation,
Compassion, and Love 58

CHAPTER FOUR
Our Children Are Not Us 63

Us and Them 64

Relinquishing the Need to Control 68

Your Ex Is Not Your Children's Ex 71

Holding Space 72

CHAPTER FIVE

Mind Full versus Mindful 75

The Mind as Storyteller 77

Mindfulness Is Mind Training 78

Mindfulness and Recovery 81

Emotional Contagion Is Bilateral 81

Mindfulness as an Operating System Upgrade 82

Mindfulness Improves Emotional Intelligence 83

Changing the Structure of Your Experience 85

N. O. A. H. S. 87

CHAPTER SIX

Meditation and Other Specific Mindfulness Practices 89

What's the Difference between Meditation
and Mindfulness? 89

Intentional Breathing 90

Meditation 93

Mini-Mindfulness Practices 97

Mindful Eating 98

Mindful Walking 100

Urge Surfing for Recovery Maintenance 102

The Paradox of Suffering 103

Mindfulness and Self-Compassion 104

Mindfulness Practice and Values 105

Practice Is a Noun as Well as a Verb 106

CHAPTER SEVEN

Connection through Communication: Part I 107

    Communication Principles 109

    Communication Skills Start with Listening 112

    Obstacles to Listening 113

    Listening and Multitasking 114

    Listening in the Face of Strong Emotions 114

CHAPTER EIGHT

Connection through Communication: Part II 117

    Ingredients for Active Listening 117

    Encouraging 119

    Asking Questions with Intention 119

    Reflecting Feelings 121

    Validating 122

    Speaking so Your Kids Will Listen 124

CHAPTER NINE

Reconciling Love and Limits 129

    Kids Have a Developmental Need for Structure
    and Limits 130

    The Therapeutic Value of Saying "No" 132

    Styles of Parenting 134

    Assign Your Children Chores 137

    Proactive Positive Attention 137

    Providing Structured Choices 138

    Setting and Enforcing Limits 140

    The Complications of Codependency 145

    A Word (or a Few) on Physical Discipline 147

    Dealing with Teenagers 149

CHAPTER TEN
Screen Media Matters 155

    A Proliferating Predicament 157

    A Manifestation of Addiction? 158

    Screen Dependence 161

    Recommendations 162

    Adults Are Not Excluded 164

CHAPTER ELEVEN
The Twelve Steps and Mindful Parenting 167

    Spiritual, Not Religious 168

    Step One 168

    Step Two 169

    Step Three 170

    Step Four 171

    Step Five 172

    Step Six 173

    Step Seven 174

    Step Eight 175

    Step Nine 176

    Step Ten 179

    Step Eleven 180

    Step Twelve 181

CHAPTER TWELVE
A Question of Balance 185

    Pain Is Inevitable; Suffering Is Optional 186

    Cognitive Consonance 188

    Emotional Equilibrium 189

    Physical Fitness 190

Spiritual Centeredness 194

Perfectly Good Enough 199

APPENDIX
Research-Documented Benefits of Mindfulness
and Meditation 203

ACKNOWLEDGMENTS

There are many people who contributed directly and indirectly to bringing *Roots and Wings* from conception to fruition, and my heartfelt appreciation extends to all of them.

To my advance readers, Beth Kovac Mager, my beautiful (inside and out) and relentlessly supportive wife, and Margie Williams, MA, LPC, dear friend and colleague, whose path and mine have so much in common.

To Central Recovery Press, for recognizing the importance of this topic and publishing *Roots and Wings.*

To Michelle Estes, my lead editor, whose guidance was instrumental in making this a better book.

To my siblings, Andy, Amy, and Ellen, whom I have come to appreciate more than they know.

To Jimmy Smith, an inspirational example of how to walk through parental minefields with mindful awareness.

To my inner support circle, Paul Hinshaw, Tony Macias, Debbie Champine, Heidi Buckley, Cisco Melendez, Johan Aleseo, Tony Carter, Tam Macanas, Alvin Elliot, Travis Shephard. Wayne Zespy, Tommy Crooks, Marcy and Ken Poreda, and Hank Greenberg.

To my brothers from the Malibu Men's Spiritual Retreat, especially, Seth Jaffe, Ronnie Ressner, Richard Frankel, George Mangual, Mi'kal Royster, Dwight Smith, Kevin Tavares, John Long, Steve Merker, John Salamon, Joe Yalich, Nick Lenderman,

Dave Skelton, Van Vee, Jeff Schnapper, Chuck Galvin, Gilbert Davalos, Tony Smith, Anthony Persiano, John Martin, Bob Grier, Vince Glisson, Jordan Kislak, Luigi Lamberto, Vinnie Kay, Michael Farrell, Alan Trevor, Roy Bowman, Christo Rein, Robin Kirsch, and Brian Fitzpatrick.

To my esteemed endorsers, Jennifer Kunst, PhD, John Bruna, Toni Bernhard, Peter Kuhn, Mel Pohl, MD, DFASAM, Greg Pergament, and Claudia Black, PhD, who thought highly enough of this book to provide their kindhearted support and generous praise.

My gratitude runs deep.

INTRODUCTION

Accomplish the great task by a series of small acts.

Lao Tzu, Tao Te Ching, Verse 63

Parenting is among the most important and complex of all human activities, yet it requires no advance preparation or training of any kind. Whether planned or unplanned, by chance or by choice, virtually anyone can become a parent.[1] Parenting presents a continuum of emotional intensity and stress that often juxtaposes indescribable love and joy with gut-wrenching heartache and fear. Many parents—especially those who are new but also those with plenty of experience—become overwhelmed by the all-encompassing nature of their responsibilities.

During my Masters in Social Work program in the late 1980s, I was introduced to a number of psychological and clinical assessment models, all of which had significant merit, yet I found myself intuitively drawn to a simple, though elegant and less well-known, model for assessing people's current status, the problems and challenges they faced, and their potential for growth and

---

1   A note on language: for simplicity and clarity, I use the terms *parent* and *parents*, but these are meant to encompass all adults who, by choice, necessity, or default, assume the roles and responsibilities of parents/primary caregivers. This often relates to grandparents or other adult family members but can also include adults with no biological relationship to the children they parent.

achievement of their identified goals. This straightforward paradigm focused on three areas: motivation, capacity, and opportunity.

1. How *motivated* are they—how important are their goals and how much effort are they willing to invest—to grow and achieve their goals?

2. What is their current *capacity*—their level of awareness, competence, and skill—to grow and achieve their goals?

3. To what extent do they have the *opportunity*—access to the circumstances that make it possible—to grow and achieve their goals?

If you're reading this, you are demonstrating considerable motivation to become a better parent to your child(ren). Opportunities to become a more attuned and skilled parent require time and energy, and while available time and energy varies widely based on individual circumstances, anyone with enough motivation can create more opportunities to further develop his or her parenting skills.

Among my core beliefs is that in every situation, people do the best they can, based on their current capacity. When we stay actively engaged in the process of recovery, our capacity expands; it becomes greater, enhancing our conscious access to resources—both internal and external—and making more options and possibilities available to us.

The awareness and skills I've learned and applied through eleven-plus plus years in recovery along with more than thirty years of daily meditation and other mindfulness practices merge with nearly two decades of professional behavioral health experience to equip me to be a better parent to my daughters—now ages thirty and twenty-six—and to share the accumulated wisdom and guidance with you. Paying conscious attention to the information contained here and applying it through practice will help you expand your capacity to be the best parent you can be.

People want to be good parents; however, many feel unprepared for the challenges parenting throws at them under the best—to say nothing of the worst—circumstances. It's not uncommon for parents to experience wearying uncertainty about whether they've done "the right thing," obsessively second-guessing decisions made and ruminating over actions taken, saying things such as "Should I have done *that?*" "Was it the best thing to do?" "What am I supposed to do *now?*" "How do I deal with *this?*"

For people in recovery from addiction, parenting is an even more complicated and sensitive issue, fraught with deep pools of guilt, regret, and shame. The complexities of negotiating communication and expectations, establishing and maintaining boundaries, balancing love and limits, dealing with discipline, and imposing appropriate consequences are challenging for every family. However, for parents who grew up in families with dysfunction ranging from violations of trust, emotional neglect, rejection, and inconsistent and unhealthy boundaries to verbal, emotional, physical, or sexual abuse, creating consistent structure and positive discipline can be particularly difficult. For parents in recovery whose children have experienced active addiction up close and personal, such dysfunction and the impacts it has on the process of parenting can be severe. In such cases, successful parenting in recovery necessitates restoring the parent-child relationship and repairing frayed trust.

For parents who entered recovery prior to having children, the parent-child relationship may be encumbered by less baggage, but the challenges remain substantial and often daunting. Romantic relationships conclude. Marriages can end. But when you become a parent, you sign on for a lifelong relationship and the nature and obligations evolve over the course of your children's growth and development. No matter how old you and they get, your children will always be your children—and you will always be their parent.

Parenthood introduced me to an entirely new level of emotional investment, and through it I learned there is no greater love than that for my children. On the other hand, there is no greater pain than to see, hear, or feel my kids in pain and be confronted with my limitations to ease it—regardless of whether their pain is physical, emotional, or both. The agony that comes from knowing I have been a source of my children's pain only adds to the heartache.

I did not feel well-prepared for the job of parenting in the months leading up to the birth of my first daughter. Even though I was not especially young (twenty-eight) and despite (or in part because of) having some knowledge of child development, part of me was terrified and intimidated by the immensity of the responsibilities that lay ahead, and another part was deeply ambivalent about the anticipated sacrifices and trade-offs. And she was planned! I truly believe one of the reasons nine months exist between conception and birth is so parents-to-be have that time to wrap their hearts and minds around the reality that their lives will be irreversibly changed.

Those who say having a child is like walking around with your heart outside of your body know exactly what they are talking about. Unfortunately, an abundance of love and the best of intentions do not in and of themselves translate to healthy, skillful parenting. All of us bring a certain amount of baggage to our parenting efforts: our genetic constitution; our innate temperament and personality; experiences with our own parents; our ability to think and process information; how we relate to and express emotions; our beliefs, habits, and conditioning; our level of self-care; our capacity for self-awareness and self-calming; and the extent to which we are "comfortable in our own skin." Weighted down by this baggage, it's not uncommon for parents to get stuck operating on unconscious habitual autopilot with their kids—reacting automatically and unskillfully over and over again, wanting to be better but not knowing how.

As I wrote in *Some Assembly Required: A Balanced Approach to Recovery and Chronic Pain*, by the time I found my way to recovery in late 2006 my daughters were nineteen and fourteen, respectively, and although all parents can, and often do, unintentionally act in ways that cause some degree of harm to their children, those of us whose children were around during our active addiction bear an extra burden. I've made many mistakes, both before and after finding my way to recovery. I continue to be a perfectly imperfect parent. Fortunately, in parenting as in recovery—and in life—it's about progress rather than perfection. There have been and continue to be occasions when my daughters have been my teachers as much as I have been theirs. Increasingly, I have learned to recognize, appreciate, and embrace those lessons.

Wanting to be a good parent, however, doesn't lead to that outcome any more than the wish to stay clean will keep people in recovery. Though some people take to it more naturally than others, healthy and attuned parenting is a learned skill. Becoming a quality parent doesn't happen by accident or coincidence either; it necessitates conscious awareness and ongoing intentional effort.

After people have a bit of time in recovery under their belts, one of the biggest challenges is balance: achieving and maintaining balance within and among four primary life domains—mental, emotional, physical, and spiritual—as well as the areas of ongoing recovery, job/career, family, friends, and other interests.

Those in recovery from addiction are frequently advised to make their recovery the highest priority, to place it "above all else." As a result, it can seem as if the needs of personal recovery and the responsibilities of parenting compete and inherently conflict. This is a false dichotomy. While at first glance recovery and parenting may seem like two distinctly different spheres, the truth is, sustaining a quality recovery program and parenting successfully overlap in many areas.

To say that being a parent can be difficult is a dramatic understatement. It's no surprise that so many parents struggle so mightily in this role. It's remarkable how many parents, including those who are successful in other important areas of their lives (perhaps most notably, their careers), often feel unskillful when it comes to parenting and their interactions with their children. And yet, as formidable as the demands of being a parent can be, if you are a person in recovery from addiction you already possess both unique understanding and valuable experience in addressing profound life challenges and responding to them with a degree of skill and success.

Roots and Wings details how recovery and parenthood can inform and enrich one another to create a synergy in which the whole far exceeds the sum of its parts. It presents a framework for skillful parenting grounded in the principles and practices of twelve-step-oriented recovery and mindfulness practices along with elements of psychological/developmental theory, contemporary counseling approaches, and a touch of neuroscience.

This book will help you sort through your baggage and choose to get rid of that which no longer serves you, so you can parent from the perspective of an emotionally lighter—and more enlightened—person. My objective is to weave together the process of recovery and mindfulness practices with the desire to be a quality parent—a good father or good mother. That being said, this is a guide for all parents, not just those in recovery from addiction.

Parallel process is an elemental thread woven throughout the tapestry of this book, and it occurs when we learn information and acquire skills for ourselves that we then transmit to others—directly and indirectly, consciously and unconsciously. The many facets of awareness and skills presented here are for you to learn and practice, so you can enhance your parenting and recovery (though, of course, they are applicable to many areas of life). This will benefit both you and your children.

As you continue to practice, a parallel process will occur naturally between you and your children. You will teach the skills you have learned to your children indirectly by modeling those skills, and as you become adept and comfortable with your newfound competencies, you can help your children learn more directly by consciously teaching these skills and encouraging your children to practice them. Developing and applying mindful awareness will help them be more skillful and content in life. And, isn't that among our most fervent hopes for our children? An added bonus is that whenever we teach something to others—no matter what it is—the experience of imparting our knowledge and skill always enhances and deepens our own awareness and understanding.

With conscious effort, old habits and thought processes can be discarded and replaced with new, healthier habits and processes. Yet, one thing that cannot be replaced is time. Time is perhaps the only thing in life that is truly irreplaceable. Our time may be the greatest gift we can give; however, time with our children is a strange phenomenon. The days—especially the arduous ones—can feel oppressively long, while the years are often unexpectedly short. Time never runs away from us as fast as it does when we view it through the lens of our children's growth and development. In the blink of an eye, they go from infants to toddlers to starting school to entering middle school to graduating high school and on to college or the world of work and then to full-on adulthood.

May this book give you the knowledge and skills to make the most of the time you have with your kids—to become the parent you want to be, the parent your kids (even if they are now adults) need you to be, and maybe even the parent you needed when you were growing up.

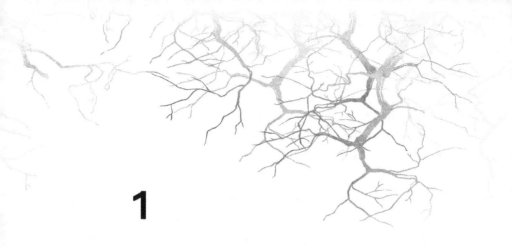

1

RECOVERY, PARENTING, AND MINDFULNESS, OH MY

It is in the shelter of each other that the people live.

Irish Proverb

At first glance, the respective provinces of recovery and parenting seem to have little in common and even less to connect them. But in fact, there are many parallels between these two seemingly disparate areas, and understanding them can enhance the quality of your parenting and recovery.

Recovery is a process of ongoing learning, growth, and healing. Similarly, parenting is also a process of learning and growth, and when it's conducted mindfully, with conscious awareness, it can also be profoundly healing.

Anticipating the birth of my first daughter, whenever I became submerged in thinking about the formidable demands and difficulties inherent in being a parent, my pulse rate quickened and my breathing became more rapid and shallow. Even though becoming a parent was a conscious choice, I was also mired in mixed emotions and even resentful about giving up the freedoms and disposable income that accrue to DINKs (double-income-no-kids). What I had no real clue about were the remarkable joys and the immersive love that awaited me.

Similarly, finding myself in addiction treatment after using mind- and mood-altering substances daily for over thirty years and knowing that I needed to enter recovery, part of me was terrified and intimidated by the idea of changing my life so dramatically, and another part was ambivalent and resentful about having to give up my primary coping mechanism, constant confidante, and long-term lover. I had no real sense of the unexpected gifts that recovery would confer and the myriad ways in which it would enrich my life. Ambivalence is intrinsic to every major life decision—those tectonic plate-shifting choices that forever alter the course of our lives. Being in conscious contact with that ambivalence and allowing oneself to feel it without becoming overwhelmed and immobilized by it is healthy. As positive as they may be, getting married, buying one's first house, relocating across considerable distances, having kids, and entering recovery all involve palpable trade-offs, costs, and benefits as well as advantages and disadvantages that naturally and normally engender ambivalence. Anyone in the throes of such immense transitions who cannot acknowledge the existence of mixed emotions is either in denial or full of shit.

Leaving behind everything we know to take on new and different life experiences is a tremendous challenge laden with uncertainty, stress, anxiety, confusion, and fear, even under the most promising circumstances. It takes strength and courage to venture beyond our existing frame of reference. Most people choose to stay inside their particular boxes of familiarity and emotional safety out of fear related to the uncertainty of the unknown. Yet, going beyond that which we already know is often the greatest generator of learning and growth.

Both recovery and parenting involve significant losses, as well as forever life-altering gains. Both are transformative and can transport us light years beyond our previous knowledge, understanding, and life experience, forcing us to go beyond the bounds of our familiarity-constrained comfort zones in profound, growth-enhancing ways.

Working a program of recovery turns out to be one of the greatest gifts a parent can give his or her children. When applied with mindful attention and intention, recovery-supporting principles and practices become resources that not only improve the well-being and functioning of the person in recovery, but they also facilitate healthy, quality parenting. Recovery infused with mindfulness gives the gift of presence (in contrast to presents), a gift that improves the well-being of children *and* their parents. Attuned and skillful parenting is the actualizing of many of the most essential spiritual principles of twelve-step recovery: acceptance, loving-kindness, patience, open-mindedness, tolerance, compassion (including self-compassion), humility, forgiveness (self-forgiveness, too), empathy, gratitude, service, and faith.

Reframing Karma

Like the path of recovery, the process of making progress in parenting is anything but linear. Under the best of circumstances, it often feels like two steps forward and one step back. The popular understanding of karma is "what goes around comes around." However attractive the concept of such poetic justice may be, it is a misconception. From a Buddhist perspective, karma destines us to have the same types of experiences (albeit perhaps in somewhat different forms) until we learn the lessons they have to teach us. The process of making progress in both recovery and parenting is reminiscent of a spiral wherein we continually come back to experiences we thought we understood and discover deeper lessons.

It's not unlike the process of dyeing cloth. Let's say that you want to change the color of a piece of white cloth to dark forest green. If you are new to this process, you might well expect that as soon as the cloth hits the dye it will turn the desired color. Such expectations are a set-up for confusion and disappointment: The first time the cloth is put into the dye it may barely change color, but each time the cloth comes in contact with the dye, the color becomes slightly deeper and richer. The desired results are attained only by putting the cloth into the dye over and over and over again.

In parenting, as in recovery from addiction, there are no magic bullets, no quick fixes, and no universally effective formulaic recipes for success in negotiating the wide range of inevitable challenges. However, there are many beneficial practices and approaches that can make a meaningful difference by helping you improve your awareness and skills in both parenting and recovery, and they involve mindfulness. Some are interactional and relate to what happens between parents and children, while others are internal and specific to parents' own mental, emotional, physical, and spiritual equilibrium—your thought process and your relationship to your thoughts, emotions, physical status, and spiritual centeredness.

The internal and interactional are intimately connected. To paraphrase both Ram Dass and Pema Chödrön, I work on myself as a way to improve my parenting, and I work on my parenting as a way to improve myself. The wisdom of this dialectic translates easily to my recovery as well: I work on myself as a way to improve my recovery, and I work on my recovery as a way to improve myself.

Suiting Up and Showing Up

If you've attended twelve-step meetings you may have heard people share about "suiting up and showing up." This saying usually refers to following through on commitments and responsibilities, even when we don't feel like it, it's inconvenient, or we just don't fucking want to. Among the most hurtful things parents can do to their children is to promise to be someplace or to do something and fail to follow through.

When young children are subjected to this hurt, it is an emotional abandonment that bludgeons their sense of trust in the world as a reliable and emotionally safe place. For older children, adolescents, and young adults, such experiences chip away at their ability to trust their parent(s) specifically, but their overall sense of trust is also adversely affected, and the impact is cumulative. At a certain point, it's irrelevant whether or not the reasons for such parental nonfeasance are reasonable or valid. Each time parents are unable to be "there" for their kids consistent with commitments made, the wounds become a little deeper, the damage a little more substantial.

Recovery reinforces the value of "suiting up and showing up" in all aspects of our lives. Most people think of this in terms of physical presence—literally showing up where and when we need to and have committed to. But it's also about being fully present and available—mentally, emotionally, and spiritually, as well as physically. Nowhere is this more critical than in parenting.

During my younger daughter's final semester in college, her mother and I were both pained and concerned about some of her struggles. With her mother 1,500 miles away, I made eight trips over the course of three months from where I live in Las Vegas to Flagstaff, Arizona, to ensure my daughter had the emotional and practical support she needed. Being there for her in this way involved driving 249 miles on Friday evening or Saturday morning and sleeping on a couch definitely not designed to be slept on with my chronic back pain, before driving 249 miles home on Sunday. It was arduous and exhausting—and I was grateful to be able to do it.

While some people might see a patina of codependency in my actions, to me they were simply what my daughter needed and deserved. Balanced recovery and attuned parenting don't provide safety *from* the storm; they increase safety *during* the storm. Moreover, depending upon the degree to which our active addiction affected our children and our relationship with them, suiting up and showing up for them in every form we can is part of an ongoing, living amends.

Actualizing the Serenity Prayer

Twelve step-oriented recovery utilizes the dialectic of *acceptance* and *change* (as do certain psychotherapeutic approaches, such as Dialectical Behavior Therapy and Acceptance and Commitment

Therapy), recognizing the therapeutic value of accepting one's current status *and* moving toward healthy change to generate learning, growth, and healing. This may seem counterintuitive, and it's natural to have questions about it. *Wait a minute!* you might think. *Aren't acceptance and change two completely different things? If I accept something, I take it as it is. I'm not trying to change it. And if I'm working to change something, by definition I'm not accepting it. WTF?!*

Dialectical thinking views all things as interconnected; even elements that may seem to contradict one another share a relationship. It's a dynamic process wherein apparent opposites move toward an integration that brings them into harmony and creates a greater whole. As Carl Jung put it, "We cannot change anything until we accept it." This is the dialectic embedded in the Serenity Prayer, and it applies elegantly to parenting, as well as to recovery:

> *Grant me the serenity*
> *to accept the things I cannot change;*
> *the courage to change the things I can;*
> *and the wisdom to know the difference.*

Everything we encounter in life ultimately breaks down into two categories: things we can change or at least have some influence over and things we can't change or influence. Whenever I take the time and make the space to consider it consciously, all of my experiences, both internal and external, fit into one of these two basic categories.

Simply recognizing in which group a challenge—be it physical, mental, emotional, spiritual, or interactional—belongs to makes my life more manageable. Beyond that, if the challenge is something I cannot change, such as the actions or attitude of another person, I need to accept it, and the issue becomes how best to facilitate that acceptance. If, on the other hand, the challenge is something I *can* change (how I'm dealing with that other person), the issue is about what I need to change and how to most effectively make it happen. One thing I can always change (as difficult as it can be at times) is how I respond to that which I cannot change.

I can change little about my daughters, especially now that they're fully formed adults with their own lives. At the time of this writing, my younger daughter lives in Las Vegas, in close proximity to me. I'd love to see her more often than I do, and it saddens me that I don't get to spend more time with her. I also know that living in Vegas is time-limited for her, and I'm blessed to see her with some regularity. So, I have a choice: to allow my reactions to be unconsciously held captive by feelings of disappointment, sadness, frustration, and/or upset that I don't see her more or practice responding with the conscious awareness that the time we spend together is precious and gratitude that I get to see her as often as I do.

That is not to suggest I dismiss or deny my distressing emotions. In between the extremes of attachment to our emotions such that they overwhelm us, and avoidance of them because they're so painful, lies a middle path. I strive to practice the mindfulness skill of observing these feelings, allowing them, and being present with them. And when I do, uncomfortable emotions become a little lighter and easier to bear.

There is a direct correlation between the choice I make and the quality of time my daughter and I spend together. Where you choose to focus your attention—a choice that is discussed at length in Chapters Five and Six—grows bigger and stronger in your mind, exerting pervasive influence on your thought process and your emotional state. As my dear friend, brother in recovery, and mindfulness teacher John Bruna describes in his wonderful book, *The Wisdom of a Meaningful Life: The Essence of Mindfulness*, we can choose to water the "flowers" or the "weeds" of our experience. As Seth Jaffe, another dear friend in long-term recovery and former interventionist featured on A&E's *Intervention*, puts it, "The grass is always greener when you water it."

Acceptance is not only a core principle of recovery, it's one of the cornerstones of mindfulness practice. With acceptance, even when it is begrudging (and sometimes it is), we give ourselves the opportunity to meet reality where it is instead of residing in a chronic state of dissatisfaction created by attachment to the idea that things should be different than they are. Some of the greatest emotional pain comes from mobilizing and maintaining resistance to things as they are. Acceptance does not mean we have to like what is happening—far from it. It simply means we stop fighting against the reality of what *is* and move toward peacefully coexisting with it. In twelve-step recovery, this is framed as *living life on its own terms*. For most people, this shift frees a remarkable amount of time and energy.

Step One of the Twelve Steps can provide a helpful frame of reference, as well as a powerful exemplar of this dynamic. After fighting against it for decades, in finally accepting the reality that I was an addict, I experienced a strange and unexpected sense of freedom. It felt as though I was able to exhale more fully than I had in a very long time. Consider what it was like when you accepted the reality of your addiction. How long and how hard had you fought against that reality? How much time and energy had you spent denying, avoiding, and otherwise struggling against it? And to what extent did you experience a sense of relief or even liberation upon coming to terms with it?

Parenting as Service

Parenting is one of the ultimate forms of *service*. Being of service is an important part of twelve-step-program participation, where the intent is to give to others in the same way that others have given to us. Service is the spiritual principle at the heart of Step Twelve: making intentional contributions to the quality of one's environment that can take many different forms, such as being of service to one's twelve-step fellowships, families, friends, organizations, neighborhoods, and communities.

Preparing your children to meet the mental, emotional, physical, and spiritual challenges of life is a monumental piece of service. As imperfectly as I have fulfilled it, parenting has been the most important service commitment I've ever had and ever will have.

A Quality Holding Environment

D.W. Winnicott, a British pediatrician turned psychoanalyst, was the first to describe the importance of a responsive "holding environment." Winnicott viewed relationships and interactions with other people, along with how individuals saw themselves vis-à-vis their most important relationships, as *the* key factor in healthy development. A quality holding environment nurtures a sense of emotional and physical safety; of being understood and accepted in ways that encourage learning and growth and promote the development of self-acceptance, resiliency, distress tolerance, and emotional self-regulation. It brings about these effects through consistency, reliability, attunement to needs, compassion, and empathy. By generating the experience of being emotionally "held" in these ways, this type of environment facilitates healthy physical, mental, emotional, and spiritual development.

The original concept of a holding environment was specific to the physical and psychological relationship and interactions between children (beginning in infancy) and their primary caregivers. Subsequently, Winnicott extrapolated the holding environment paradigm to the relationship and interactions between therapist and client, wherein part of the therapist's role is to create an environment that assists clients' growth and healing. The holding environment concept has since been applied to the relationship and quality of interaction between parents and their children more generally, as well as to the family as a whole, in addition to other settings, such as schools, recreational programs, spiritual/religious communities, and various other systems of social and emotional support.

So, parents provide the first and most critical holding environment. But if you don't have much frame of reference for a healthy holding environment, drawing on your experience in twelve-step recovery can be of great value. Early on in my recovery, I realized that twelve-step fellowships can and often do provide a responsive and effective holding environment. My twelve-step fellowship creates the space where people can feel safe enough to allow themselves to become vulnerable, talking openly and honestly about the most sensitive aspects of their lives, including secrets kept carefully guarded and possibly never shared with anyone previously.

Although it's best for the growth and development of children to have a healthy holding environment from birth, it's beneficial for both you and your children to move toward providing this experience whenever you can. If, for whatever reasons, you haven't been able to create and sustain one before, you can begin now.

Hugs Not Drugs

In my twelve-step fellowship, we greet each other with a hug. Whenever I see my daughters, we hug. I'm not talking about a fleeting, drive-by, pat-on-the-back-style hug, but rather one that is substantial, sustained, and heartfelt. Hugging another person with intention and feeling is a powerful form of recognition, an unequivocal acknowledgement that he or she *matters*. It is an indicator of intimacy that says, "I got you," even—or perhaps especially—in the face of adversity.

Physiologically, hugging precipitates the release of oxytocin, often referred to as the "bonding hormone" because it promotes attachment and strengthens existing bonds and relationships, which includes the bond between mothers and their newborn babies. Oxytocin is a chemical of interpersonal connection not only released through physical closeness with another person but also through other forms of bonding, such as eye contact, smiling, and attentiveness.

In addition to such psychological sustenance, hugging also provides significant health benefits, starting with its stress reducing, calming effects. Recent research demonstrates that oxytocin is associated with decreases in the stress hormones cortisol and norepinephrine, as well as increased levels of the feel-good neurotransmitters dopamine and serotonin (the body's natural antidepressant that is also involved in mood regulation). There's also evidence that hugs and the oxytocin release that accompanies them reduce heart rate and blood pressure, increase feelings of well-being, and improve immune system function and pain tolerance.[2]

A Brief Introduction to Mindfulness

If you're not intimately familiar with *mindfulness*, it may seem like a trendy new fad. In recent years, it has become increasingly discussed in mainstream circles in the United States, including in business settings. However, the ancient wisdom of mindfulness and its practices actually originated approximately 2,700 years ago, arising from the spiritual traditions of Taoism in China around 600 BCE and Buddhism in India around 500 BCE.

Mindfulness refers to the conscious awareness of one's present experience—internal (thoughts, emotions, and physical sensations) and external (people, places, and circumstances)—with acceptance and without judgment. It involves paying attention with the intent to observe and accept the ongoing unfolding of your current experience without becoming overidentified with or attached to the content of thoughts, emotions, and sensory experiences.

Through mindfulness and its associated practices, including meditation (part of the foundation of Step Eleven), people develop greater present-moment awareness, learn to direct and keep their attention where they want it, and develop the capacity to face uncomfortable, painful thoughts, feelings, and physical sensations— learning how to accept the pain, anxiety, anger, or sadness and let it pass—without obsessing on those experiences or needing to change them. This set of skills is especially important in our increasingly technology-driven culture with its twenty-four-seven connectivity and greater demands on our precious time, energy, attention, and emotional availability.

A testament to the therapeutic value of mindfulness is that more and more medical and behavioral health professionals incorporate mindfulness practices into their approaches to helping people. Acceptance and Commitment Therapy, Dialectical Behavior

---

2   Stacey Colino, "The Health Benefits of Hugging," *US News & World Report* (February 3, 2016) http://health.usnews.com/health-news/health-wellness/articles/2016-02-03/the-health-benefits-of-hugging.

Therapy, Mindfulness-Based Cognitive Therapy, and Mindfulness-Based Stress Reduction all draw on mindfulness practices. Mindfulness-based protocols have also been developed for relapse prevention of addictive behaviors.

Trail Finding and Following

As an avid hiker, I've found hiking in wilderness areas to be an excellent metaphor for the processes of recovery and parenting. It's an activity that also necessitates and promotes mindfulness. Following a trail in the mountains, forest, or desert provides valuable experiences and opportunities to learn and practice skills that apply to all three arenas. When the trail is wide and well defined, I can see what lies ahead for a considerable distance. When the route is fraught with twists and turns, it is impossible to know what's around the next bend. Sometimes a trail starts out easy to identify and follow, but later, the very same trail becomes difficult to discern, seeming to disappear altogether or present several potential—and equally plausible—options.

Under such circumstances, I've found it best to pause and become still physically and mentally. When I become more mindful in observing and quieting the internal chatter that drives anxiety, frustration, and self-doubt, I'm able to pay closer and more attuned attention, locate the trail, and continue. Occasionally my assessment of where the trail picks up is mistaken and I have to backtrack to find the correct path.

Sometimes the terrain is nice and level, or has mild uphills and downhills, and is easy to traverse. At other times it's brutally steep, necessitating significant ascents and subsequent descents, making the trek arduous and wearying. The steep inclines are often slow, require tremendous energy, and are hardest on the muscles, while steep downhills necessitate continuous adjustments to maintain balance and place great stress on the joints. Sometimes, the trail is smooth and relatively free of obstacles, or it's covered with large rocks or loose rock known as *scree*, tree roots, or deep sand, making it challenging to negotiate, and a misplaced step can lead to falls and injuries.

Some trails can seem routine and prosaic, their inherent beauty more commonplace and subtle, and I have to look harder and deeper to see it. Other trails traverse such remarkable landscapes that their beauty smacks me upside the head and instills an electric wonder. Some days on the trail are a slog. My body is heavy and lethargic, and each step seems difficult. Progress is slow and halting as I plod forward, narrowing my focus to placing one foot in front of the other, literally taking everything one step at a time. Other days, my mind and body are in tune, and my spirit is open wide, synced with the wind caressing stands of Ponderosa Pines, Douglas Firs, and (above 9,000 feet in elevation in select areas of southern Nevada) Bristlecone Pines, along with the faces of granite, sandstone, and limestone rock formations.

For me, hiking is a consistently challenging experience that necessitates careful and conscious preparation, as well as a tremendous amount of work. The tradeoff? Being able to see and experience wondrous, transcendent places—geographically and spiritually—that open my heart and are accessible in no other way. The same is true for both recovery and parenting.

Perfection Is Bullshit

To be in recovery is to have known great pain. Being a parent is to know great pain. My daughters kill me softly in a thousand ways, and I know that I have hurt them deeply. After more than a decade in recovery, there are still moments when I get entangled in longing that the narrative of my story had unfolded differently, when I ruminate on choice points and what might have been, and I'm enmeshed with a piercing sense of the loss and grief that still seeps from it. However, I know the pain and anguish of significant loss is an inexorable part of being human. None of us is exempted from that experience, whether or not we know the ravages of active addiction or the special heartbreaks of parenting.

It is only when I consciously recognize and make peace with the darkness and pain within myself that I can be fully present with the darkness and pain of others, including my children. Recovery infused with mindfulness is a process of learning and building the skills of identifying and feeling our emotions, rather than avoiding, numbing, or escaping them. For better or worse, the only way we can experience the best, the deepest, and the most exquisitely intimate connections in life is to soften our hearts in ways that make us vulnerable to the greatest hurt. We don't get one without the possibility of the other (fuck). Nowhere is this reality more apparent than in the arena of romantic partnerships and parenting.

There is no such thing as perfect recovery. And there's no such thing as perfect parenting—not even close. The only way to go through either process is thoroughly imperfectly. Your children will experience their share of emotional pain, and often there is little you can do to prevent it or take it away. Inevitably, you will be the source of some of your children's emotional pain. That's simply the way it works. Parent-child interactions are so complex and psychologically charged that no matter what most people do or don't do as parents it provides potential fodder for their children's future psychotherapy.

Realistically, the best we can do is learn how to more consistently bring to bear a balanced approach—leaning into the challenges of parenthood with conscious awareness, presence, and skill while practicing self-compassion, self-acceptance, and self-forgiveness when our imperfections inevitably rear their heads and we fall short of our ideals.

"Seat" is a term used in the equestrian world to describe one's balance and ability to sit and successfully remain seated in the saddle under variable and often unpredictable circumstances. Recovery combined with mindfulness creates a powerful vehicle for keeping your seat (maintaining your balance), no matter what parenthood may throw at you.

Putting the Pieces Together

Achieving and sustaining progress on any meaningful path of change—such as recovery and parenting—is analogous to the process of constructing furniture purchased in "knock-down" or ready-to-assemble form. For instance, when you need a new desk and purchase one from IKEA, it comes in a large box that contains many different parts. Some of these parts are familiar, while others may be completely alien to you.

The challenge of putting these pieces together to create the desk you want and that will meet your needs can seem overwhelming. All too often, parts don't fit properly or are missing altogether, and the instructions can be so difficult to interpret that they might as well be in a foreign language (and sometimes are). Assembling the desk successfully involves negotiating negative thoughts and beliefs that feed a morass of distressing emotions such as anxiety, self-doubt/inadequacy, frustration, and anger. Progress takes place in small, halting increments. Yet one piece at a time, the desk gradually comes together to assume its intended form and function.

Recovery and parenting are infinitely more abstract and complex, but the fundamental architecture and processes are more similar than you might think. Assembling the pieces that nurture a life of meaning, contentment, and value is a continuous process. It requires identifying and gathering the necessary pieces, seeing how they fit together, and often reconfiguring them—replacing some pieces with others and rearranging them to create the most functional and healthy fit. This fit is individualized; what fits beautifully for me may not be a great fit for you, and vice versa. Sometimes we put the pieces together and they work well for a time, but at some point we may need to seek out new pieces or a different configuration to better meet our present needs.

Like recovery, parenting is a process rather than an outcome—a journey as opposed to a destination. More accurately, in both recovery and parenting, the journey *is* the destination. As Ram Dass expressed so beautifully, "We are all just walking each other home."

2

ROOTS THEN WINGS

*If you realize that all things change,
there is nothing you will try to hold on to.*

Lao Tzu, *Tao Te Ching*, Verse 74

My professional background in behavioral health crystallized my awareness that when we do our jobs as parents well, we give our kids roots, and then we help them grow wings. Roots provide a stable and solid attachment that connects parents and their children— a secure foundation from which children can grow and develop.

In twelve-step recovery, we make a commitment to abstain from alcohol and other drugs, no matter what. Creating a secure base for children requires parental commitment to being attuned and taking action in ways that promote safety, security, and trust—no matter what. Children develop a sense of safety, security, and trust through consistency, reliability, and stability on the part of their parents. Such commitment involves devotion to cultivating and maintaining the soil in which our children's roots grow, making it soft, receptive, and fertile by

- providing consistent physical and emotional protection;

- being responsive to our children's individual needs and interests;

- showing our children kindness, compassion, and empathy;

- providing appropriate structure—setting and enforcing boundaries, limits, and consequences.

Wings equip children to separate and individuate from their parents and *become*—taking off from that secure base toward a future of their own choosing. The solid foundation poured during early childhood becomes a runway in adolescence and young adulthood. Helping your children grow healthy wings entails

- role-modeling real-life examples of acceptance, integrity, responsibility, tolerance, honesty, humility, gratitude, forgiveness, and love;

- nurturing their physical, emotional, intellectual, and ethical development;

- encouraging their burgeoning age-appropriate autonomy.

Familiarity through Transition

Shortly after I finished my master's degree in social work—complete with some knowledge of attachment theory and child development—my first daughter was born, and one of the first items we bought for her was a small and portable lambskin rug. She slept on "Lamby" nightly, rested on it, and cuddled up with it. It went everywhere she did, providing a measure of comfort, consistency, and—most importantly—familiarity. No matter where she was, a little piece of home went with her. In the language of psychodynamic psychotherapy, Lamby was a *transitional object*, an item of psychological comfort that represented stability and consistency. Such transitional objects help young children negotiate changes in place, people, and circumstance by providing inner balance and anchoring them to a secure base.

At the age of four and a half, my daughter relinquished Lamby to her newborn sister, who enjoyed the same benefits from it as her older sister until she was about four, when I mistakenly put it in the dryer after a machine washing. This reduced Lamby to the size of a small bandana. I felt absolutely awful. My self-talk seamlessly kicked into hypercritical condemnation: *Great job, asshole. You know how important Lamby is to the kids and you fucking ruined it!* Fortunately, by that time my daughters had gotten most of what they most needed from Lamby as a transitional object.

The experience of familiarity is important for children, and the younger they are, the more important it is. Familiarity provides heightened comfort and a sense of safety and security. As a result, when children travel and visit less familiar places and people (with or without their parents) and make the transition from home to daycare, preschool, or school, anything reminiscent of "home" helps children feel more secure and at ease.

Interestingly, my inspiration for making the experience of "home" portable had little to do with my professional education or experience. It coalesced through my attendance at many dozens of Grateful Dead concerts across the United States. Early on in my tenure as a Deadhead, I noticed that the band always performed on large Persian rugs laid out on the stage, regardless of whether the venue was a small intimate music hall, such as the Warfield Theatre in San Francisco, or a massive arena, such as Madison Square Garden in New York. From what I could discern, the same rugs were used at every concert, traveling with the Dead from show to show, just like their amplifiers and instruments.

Beyond the practical benefits these rugs afforded (improving footing/traction, cushioning to reduce fatigue during extended sets, concealing wires, and attenuating the noise levels onstage so band members could more easily hear each other and stay in sync), it was fascinating to see that even to the ultimate road warriors—the Grateful Dead performed more than 2,300 concerts across the globe over their thirty years together from 1965 to 1995—this familiarity had psychological meaning and value.

Strengthening Roots through Protection and Family Rituals

Because children, especially young children, have limited abilities and internal resources, a cornerstone of parenting essential for healthy roots is providing emotional in addition to physical protection for our children. Creating and maintaining a physically and emotionally safe space is the single most important theme in the parent-child relationship. The fundamental experience of safety is critical for transformation. Children need to feel secure, held, and heard before they can take the risks necessary for growth.

When my elder daughter graduated from kindergarten, the school held a ceremony in the auditorium. The twenty some-odd students stood side by side in front of the elevated stage as they sang several songs. My daughter stood second from the left; Jody, an adorable little girl in a floral print dress, stood next to her. The parents sat in several rows of folding chairs about fifteen feet from their kids.

During the second song, Jody suddenly began to projectile vomit. A stream of puke landed two feet in front of her with a loud wet *splat* that echoed throughout the auditorium. She threw up again. And again. Incredibly, no one, neither her parents nor the school staff, made a move to assist the poor child. Staff members continued to lead the kids through the song as if nothing unusual had happened. It was surreal—everyone appeared superglued in place. My daughter's mother and I were dumbfounded, eyes wide in what-the-fuck astonishment.

Perhaps you're familiar with the contagion that can affect those in too-close-for-comfort proximity to someone who just vomited. I could see by my daughter's facial expressions that she was on the verge of getting sick herself. I got up from my seat, walked up to within a few feet of her, and motioned for her to come with me.

In spite of her tender age, the proximate puddle of puke, and her rapidly encroaching nausea, my breaking program protocol—as if the repeated vomiting hadn't already shot that to shit—embarrassed her. She tried to shoo me away, but I persisted because I knew she'd be infinitely more upset if she threw up, too. I repositioned her at the opposite end of the line of students, where she was clearly more comfortable and no longer at risk of parting with her stomach contents. Mind-numbingly, it wasn't until the song concluded that anyone attended to Jody.

Part of tilling and nurturing the soil in which children's roots can grow strong and deep is balancing love with limits: helping children learn healthy boundaries through structure that includes setting—and, as necessary, enforcing—appropriate limits. Regular family rituals that help to mitigate stress and serve as anchors of connection also facilitate the development of healthy roots. Among the most therapeutically valuable of these is the family meal.

When I was Vice President of Counseling for Jewish Family and Children's Services (JFCS) of Southern Arizona from 1997 to 2005, our clinical staff had monthly case consultations with an eminent child psychiatrist. During one of the consultations, he observed that among the children he treated, almost none of their families sat down to eat *together*. It seemed to him that family meals had become practically extinct. The simple notion of using regular family meals as a therapeutic intervention struck all of us, and subsequently our therapists used it with their clients.

Long before my time at JFCS, I committed to the practice of having regular family dinners with my wife and children. No one else seemed to accord it the value I did; my daughters intermittently pushed back and grumbled about it, even when they were younger. But, I was determined that at least once a day we would gather in the same place at the same time with minimal distraction. It was a built-in opportunity to talk about our daily lives and simply *be* with one another.

Even if the meal was fairly brief, sometimes lasting no more than twenty minutes, that time was sacrosanct. We were present—

together. Not surprisingly, as my daughters grew older, their pushback escalated, but I held my ground, and we continued to have family dinners together regularly until my eldest daughter went away to college. The three of us who remained continued the practice until their mother and I separated when my younger daughter was fifteen.

With the outsize demands of everyday life in the twenty-first century, it may seem like an impossible task to get your family together at the same time for a meal. Everyone seems to move in different directions at high speed with competing needs and interests. Kids have school, extracurricular activities, and homework. Parents have work—and sometimes school—in addition to their own outside interests and self-care priorities. Single parents are spread even more thinly, and parents in recovery have additional commitments and needs related to self-care. If you participate in a twelve-step program, time and space is required for meetings, step work, and sponsor/sponsee contact among other activities.

Despite the challenges you face, make it a priority to have family meals together at home as consistently as possible, even if it's only two or three times a week. Daily is ideal, but often life is not. Make the time and space to have meals as a family around a table, not sitting on the couch. Because creating this time and space becomes harder as children age and move into adolescence and young adulthood, parents need to give consistent messages prioritizing it. As important as having family meals is the condition that no phones or other electronic devices are allowed at the table, making family meals a phone, text, social media, and TV-free zone. This applies to everyone, including parents.

Pay attention to the quality of interaction during your family meals. Seek to make the experience as positive and nurturing as you can. This is not the time to scold your kids or eat in uneasy silence. Engage your kids in conversation. Ask them to tell you about their day: What was challenging for them? What was the best part of their day? Share some of your day with them. This is an opportunity to unplug from external distractions and plug into each other.

Beyond strengthening family bonds and improving communication, recent research demonstrates that having regular family meals has many powerful benefits for children and adolescents, including improved nutrition and a lower long-term risk of obesity.[3] Mealtime conversation improves the vocabulary of young children even more than being read to.[4]

Regular family meals are a simple and effective way to reduce adolescents' risk of using tobacco, alcohol, and other drugs, as well as improving their academic performance.[5] The more frequent the family dinners, the more children experience parental support, are committed to learning, respect boundaries, have positive values and a positive identity, and demonstrate social competencies. Moreover, more frequent family dinners also correlate with lower rates of substance use, sexual activity, depression, suicide, antisocial behaviors, violence, school problems, binge eating, and purging. These positive results are generally consistent among many different types of families across the socioeconomic spectrum.[6]

Life Is a Developmental Process

Life is an ongoing progression of growth and change that takes children from one phase or stage of development to another. Every age and stage of development has its wonders and its challenges.

One of the most highly regarded models of human development is that of Erik Erikson, a psychoanalyst and developmental psychologist. First published in his 1950 book *Childhood and Society*— and expanded and refined in later books, notably *Identity and the Life Cycle*—Erikson's framework emphasizes the impact of family and social interactions on emotional development across eight stages that traverse the entire lifespan, from infancy to old age.

---

3   Jerica M. Berge et al., "The Protective Role of Family Meals for Youth Obesity: 10-Year Longitudinal Associations," *Journal of Pediatrics* 166, no. 2: 296–301.

4   C. E. Snow and D. E. Beals, "Mealtime Talk that Supports Literacy Development," *New Directions for Child and Adolescent Development* (2006): 51–66. doi:10.1002/cd.155.

5   QEV Analytics, Ltd. And Knowledge Networks, *The Importance of Family Dinners VI*, National Center on Addiction and Substance Abuse (CASA) at Columbia University (September 2010).

6   Jayne A. Fulkerson, et al., "Family Dinner Meal Frequency and Adolescent Development: Relationships with Developmental Assets and High-Risk Behaviors," *Journal of Adolescent Health* 39, no. 3: 337–345.

According to Erikson, growth occurs as we negotiate the succession of challenges presented to us throughout our lifespan. Our sense of self continuously evolves with new experiences and information we acquire through our interactions with others. A coherent and healthy sense of self and feelings of self-efficacy come about through the meeting of developmental needs and experiences of competence, while an incomplete and inferior sense of self, along with feelings of inadequacy, result from unmet developmental needs and the absence of success.

Erikson's Stages of Psychosocial Development

Many people view each of Erikson's eight stages of psychosocial development as distinct and separate, but, in reality, these stages don't begin neatly and end cleanly; they often overlap and blend into one another. "Successful" completion of each stage results in the acquisition of critical psychological strengths and resources, which are carried into subsequent stages. Although problems in moving through a stage spill over into later stages and reduce the ability to negotiate them successfully, it is possible to complete the work of earlier stages at a later time.

These stages are universal in the sense that everyone goes through them in the same order. Although there are specific age ranges associated with each stage, these are approximate—how long people spend in each stage and how old they are when they move from one stage to the next can be different for each person. This is due in part to the often-considerable difference between a person's chronological age and how old or mature they are emotionally. Moreover, every stage of development has its significant challenges— for both children and their parents. No stage is necessarily easier or more difficult, though, for some parents, certain stages may seem easier and be preferable to others.

Every stage presents children and parents with new and different challenges. The conventional interpretation is that each culminates in a decisive stage-specific positive or negative outcome—for example, trust versus mistrust in the first stage—that sets the tone for the next stage. I think the binary nature of this perspective is too limiting, however. Rather than the stage of infancy (birth to eighteen months) leading to *either* basic trust *or* general mistrust of the world, I see them as existing on a continuum in which the result for most is somewhere in between. Between the extremes of black and white at each stage are myriad shades of gray.

The first three developmental stages (and most of the fourth) focus on the growth of children's roots. The fifth and sixth stages (adolescence and young adulthood) emphasize building and stretching children's wings.

Stage 1: Infancy (Ages Birth to 18 Months)—Trust vs. Mistrust

If an infant receives nurturing, consistent, predictable, and reliable care at this stage, he or she will develop a basic sense of trust that the world is a safe place and that others will "be there" for him or her. This sense of trust carries over to future relationships, enabling the person to feel secure even when difficulties arise.

Conversely, if the infant's care is detached, inconsistent, unpredictable, and/or unreliable, the result will be a fundamental mistrust in the world as a safe place, and the sense that personal needs will likely go unmet. This spills over into future relationships and adversely affects a person's belief that others will be there for him or her.

Stage 2: Toddlerhood (Ages 18 Months to 3 Years)—Autonomy vs. Shame and Doubt

In this stage, children develop beginning physical competencies, including learning to walk. They discover an increasing array of skills and abilities, such as manipulating toys and putting on clothes and shoes. Their burgeoning sense of self as distinct from their parents manifests through other assertions of independence: intentionally walking away from their parents, wanting to make choices as to what they eat and what clothing they wear, and—most notoriously—saying no.

Ideally, parents provide a supportive environment that encourages their children to explore their abilities and do as much as they safely can by and for themselves. Such an environment allows children the opportunity to fail and, in turn, learn from that experience. For example, whenever time and circumstances permit, attuned parents let their children attempt to dress themselves rather than automatically assuming they're unable to do it on their own and stepping in to help. Ideally, parents find the patience to allow their children to try until they either succeed or ask for help. Autonomy and skill development need to be encouraged and supported while assistance is made available as needed.

When this happens, children begin to have a sense of personal control, physical competence, and independence. When it doesn't, they doubt their skills and their ability to influence their environment, contributing to feelings of dependence and a sense of inadequacy.

Stage 3: Play Age (3 to 5 Years)—Initiative vs. Guilt

During this stage, children continue to develop independence and competence and increasingly exert influence on their environment. This occurs through ongoing interactions with other children at day care or preschool and different forms of play that provide children with opportunities to try out their interpersonal skills. Children plan activities, make up games and stories, and participate in activities with peers—both organized and informal. Ideally, they learn how to lead as well as to follow. In this period, children also closely observe the adults around them and engage in extensive imitation of their behaviors.

When children have the experience of being included and accepted in these contexts, they develop a sense of comfort in taking initiative and feelings of basic confidence in their decision-making abilities. Conversely, if children's efforts are squelched or discouraged through criticism or control, whether by adults or peers, the result is a sense of guilt and feelings of lower self-worth, of being less than others.

Stage 4: School Age (5 to 12 Years)—Industry vs. Inferiority

In this stage, also referred to as *latency age*, the world of children expands as they experience and must learn how to cope with new demands through the introduction of school and formal education. They become capable of absorbing a great deal of new knowledge and build new skills related to reading, writing, rudimentary math, and analytical thinking. Teachers assume an important role as they help children learn specific skills, and peer relationships gain greater importance and become a significant source of self-esteem.

If parents and teachers encourage and validate children's learning and accomplishments during this stage, the children's sense of competence and self-efficacy increases, and confidence in their ability to achieve goals expands. If parents, teachers, and other important adults discourage or appear unsupportive in any way, or if children experience little success in school, sports, or peer-related endeavors, feelings of inferiority and lingering doubt in their abilities arise.

Stage 5: Adolescence (Ages 12 to 19)—Identity vs. Role Confusion

Adolescence is the stage that bridges childhood and adulthood. Teenagers embark on the transition to becoming adults, attempting to define who they are as individuals and how they fit in the world. Adolescence, especially in the world today, is a complicated period of life—a time of uncertainty and confusion related to rapid physical and emotional changes and shifting expectations: expectations teenagers have of themselves, expectations they have of others, and expectations others have of them.

Developing an identity involves actively figuring out the kind of person a teenager wants to be—this includes how they see themselves and how they want others to see them. They may check out different images, effectively trying them on like different clothes to see how they fit and look using two mirrors: the one on the wall and the direct and indirect feedback they receive from their peers, parents, and others. Adolescents explore and often experiment with a variety of different values, beliefs, roles, activities, and behaviors.

Coming to terms with their sexuality and sexual orientation is a critical part of identity formation. Adolescents struggle to develop their own identities while navigating the tremendous pressure to fit in with others (friends, neighborhood, community, etc.). Such peer pressures can include using mind- and mood-altering substances, having sex, and participating in law-violating activities.

The biggest and most important developmental task faced by every adolescent is the transition from child to grown-up. Most teenagers want it both ways. On the one hand, they don't want to be treated like a kid. They want more independence and privileges, including the ability to make more decisions for themselves, which comes with being an adult. On the other hand, adulthood comes with expectations and responsibilities they're in no hurry to assume.

The process of *separation-individuation* is a natural and normal part of growing up. It involves separating from the family of origin and childhood influences enough for adolescents to figure out who they are and further become their own person. In seeking greater independence, they increasingly pull away from their families and gravitate toward their peers, which frequently causes upset and conflict for teenagers and their parents. It involves a certain amount of exploration, experimentation, risk-taking, and limit testing, as well as questioning, opposing, and sometimes saying (through both words and actions), "Screw you!" Sometimes part of this process involves using alcohol and other drugs and participating in other potentially addictive activities.

Ideally, separation-individuation is about renegotiating family relationships so that teenagers achieve more autonomy and responsibility while still maintaining a positive connection with family. In many families, however, people become so detached from each other that there is little to no positive connection. In others, family members are so closely connected to each other that separating from the family to become one's own person is extremely difficult to do. As people move toward adulthood, the goals are to become independent without being isolated and connected without remaining dependent.

Success in this stage results in a coherent identity and sense of self. Some adolescents attempt to delay their progress toward adulthood and refuse or withdraw from responsibilities. Failure to establish a sense of identity leads to role confusion regarding who they are and uncertainty about their place in society.

Stage 6: Young/Emerging Adulthood (Ages 19 to 35)—Intimacy vs. Isolation

Over the last two decades adolescence has seemingly become prolonged, now lasting into the early to mid-twenties. Consequently (although this was not part of Erikson's original formulation), the first part of this stage has, for many individuals, morphed into a continuation of the stage of adolescence, a development consistent with current scientific research indicating that the human brain doesn't fully develop until about the age of twenty-five.[7]

Recent research has also confirmed that adolescent and adult brains work differently. Adults make much greater use of the prefrontal cortex—the mature decision-making part of the brain that responds to situations with rationality, sound judgment, and an awareness of long-term consequences. Adolescents process information and make decisions primarily through the amygdala— the part of the brain responsible for emotions, emotion-related memory, and survival reactions. In the brains of teenagers and emerging adults, the connections between the amygdala and the prefrontal cortex are still very much under construction.[8]

This means society allows young people who are technically legal adults to make adult decisions without fully mature brains. Kids can drive around the age of sixteen, vote and enlist in the military at eighteen, and legally consume alcohol and gamble at twenty-one. While the people who set policy at rental car companies may not

---

7   J. N. Giedd, "Structural Magnetic Resonance Imaging of the Adolescent Brain." *Annals of the New York Academy of Sciences,* 1021 (2004): 77–85. doi:10.1196/annals.1308.009.

8   Rita Sather and Amit Shelat (reviewers), "Understanding the Teen Brain," *University of Rochester Medical Center Health Encyclopedia.* https://www.urmc.rochester.edu/encyclopedia/content. aspx?contenttypeid=1&contentid=3051.

be familiar with contemporary neuroscience, they apparently know what they're doing: you cannot rent a car until the age of twenty-five.

During this stage of development, the creation of a stable identity and sense of self continues, while the search for committed companionship and love intensifies. "I don't know what I want to be when I grow up" used to be the province of teenagers; now, not so much, as most young adults continue their quest to determine who they are and what their place in the world is well into their twenties and often into their thirties. Parents continue to have an important and evolving influence in the lives of their young adult children, who often take longer to move away from home than previous generations and are more likely to move back home at some point before relocating more permanently.

The focus in this stage is on clarifying direction related to relationships, love, and career. There may be multiple changes in residence, roommates, and romantic partners prior to transitioning toward more stability in the form of committing to long-term romantic partnerships or marriages, having children, and identifying a career path. Success in this stage means learning to share oneself authentically and intimately with others, leading to the establishment of long-term relationships outside the family of origin that results in a sense of satisfaction and commitment. Failure culminates in the avoidance of intimacy and fear of relationships and commitment and can lead to lasting loneliness and isolation.

Stage 7: Adulthood (Ages 35 to 62)—Generativity vs. Self-Absorption

This stage takes place during what might be called middle adulthood, when people assume greater responsibilities related to work, career, and family. They become established in careers, settle down within a primary relationship, and grow families. Many people also experience a need to create and nurture things that contribute to society and will outlast them.

Generativity is a term Erikson developed to mean "a concern for establishing and guiding the next generation." Actualized through raising children, becoming involved in one's community, and mentoring others, among other pursuits. Major life shifts also typically occur during this stage. Children leave home, divorce and remarriage occur, and careers change. Success leads to feelings of usefulness and accomplishment, while failure results in stagnation, a lack of purpose, and feelings of meaninglessness.

Stage 8: Senior Adulthood (Ages 62 and Older)—Integrity vs. Despair

In this final stage of development, productivity generally ebbs, and many people retire from their full-time work lives. They reflect on their life and contemplate their accomplishments or lack thereof.

Success results in integrity with regard to having lived a successful life based not on material success but on the quality of one's life in terms of character, conscientiousness, decency, and overall contentment. This leads to a sense of closure and completeness with life and a concomitant acceptance of death. On the other hand, failure results in dissatisfaction with one's life; a sense of meaninglessness; feelings of regret, depression, and despair; and a more pronounced fear of death.

Change Is the Only Constant

Gains and losses occur with each successive developmental stage. In fact, growth cannot exist without loss; like a snake shedding its outgrown skin, people grow beyond what no longer fits them. This dynamic also characterizes the process of recovery.

Our kids' need to grow wings becomes clearer during adolescence with the process of separation-individuation and continues to manifest in young adulthood. Separation-individuation, wherein kids more assertively start to develop their own identities as individuals separate from their parents, is a natural and essential part of healthy psychological development. It is part of the circle of life in action.

Yet, many parents struggle with their children's separation-individuation. Their love for their children may be undiminished, but rather than emotionally supporting their kids as they sprout wings and desire greater distance and increasing autonomy, often, consciously and unconsciously, they discourage it. As one unfortunate example, I've seen deeply caring, otherwise incredibly supportive parents encourage their kids to attend college locally rather than go away for school, and live at home rather than on campus (unrelated to financial issues)—sometimes promising to buy them a car as part of the deal—in order to keep them close.

While it's normal, understandable, and healthy for parents to feel ambivalent and sad as their children advance toward adulthood, they need to work through such emotions, separating their needs from those of their children (as hard as it may be). Parents who cannot adjust to and accept these losses do their children a great disservice.

Children pick up on these feelings and can become consciously and unconsciously influenced by them, sometimes finding ways to clip their own wings to assuage their parents' discomfort. Whenever parents are unable to deal with the losses inherent in their children's natural progression toward independence and a life of their own choosing, the development of healthy wings is inhibited.

One of the immutable realities of the universe is that everything changes all the time. Over time, our relationships, our communities, our bodies, our health, our worldviews, and our children, along with the relationship we have with our children, all change. In spite of this universal truth, we continue to expect things and people to remain the same.

This is reflected in the first law of Buddhist psychology: All phenomena are impermanent and constantly changing, yet we tend to relate to them as though they were permanent. Trying to hold onto things, or people, as they were is a futile struggle, akin to attempting to keep the tide from coming in. It is a denial of reality that generates tremendous stress and unnecessary suffering.

As the second of Buddhism's Four Noble Truths informs us, the attachment to and desire for something different from the reality of "what is" causes and exacerbates suffering. When parents cling to images and recollections of their children as they were in earlier developmental stages, rather than respect the needs and interests of their children as they evolve, they create suffering for themselves and their children. And the more parents resist their children's growth and put more effort into fighting against and denying age-appropriate changes, the more suffering they create.

This leads to another loss for parents: the opportunity to appreciate their kids as they are in each precious developmental stage, remembering that it will never come again. As Tibetan Buddhist master and teacher Anyen Rinpoche put it, "If we're not reflecting on the impermanent nature of life . . . a lot of unimportant things then seem important."[9]

When Helping Hinders

As parents, the most natural, normal, and understandable desire is to help your kids: to do everything you can to support them and be there for them in as many ways as possible. But, at what point does helping begin to hinder?

You may be familiar with the term *helicopter parents*—parents who "hover" over their kids, whose lives are enmeshed with those of their kids, and who are unable to let them go or be on their own, even for a short time.

Many parents are overinvolved in and have a need to control the lives of their children. Consider the schedules of so many children today, beginning at frighteningly young ages: playdates, soccer matches, T-ball games, music lessons, and other extracurricular activities up the yin-yang, along with rigorous expectations for academic performance and perhaps tutoring to help improve that performance. Individually, these are all helpful and healthy, but when packaged together, overscheduled and overstimulated children result. They create stress and anxiety for both child and parents. Moreover, they don't allow enough space for down time and leave too little time and energy available for free play, where children have to use their own internal and interactional resources in the process

---

9   Anyen Rinpoche and Allison Choying Zangmo, *Living and Dying with Confidence: A Day-by-Day Guide* (Massachusetts: Wisdom Publications, 2016).

of practicing and strengthening their problem-solving and decision-making capabilities. For many kids, this sort of highly structured, unrelenting schedule, sky-high expectations, and attendant stress and anxiety continue through high school and often follow them through college.

A core characteristic that contributes to addiction is the sense of internal emptiness—a feeling of being empty, hollow, that something is missing. Alcohol and other drugs, in addition to other manifestations of addiction (gambling, sex, food, etc.), serve the purpose of temporarily filling that void. Overinvolvement in the lives of your children is also a way of trying to fill that hole. Recovery teaches us that attempts to fill this internal emptiness with external "things" never work for long. Mindfulness teaches us that we can become consciously aware of this feeling, be present with it, and learn to peacefully coexist with and accept it, without needing to sate it.

Similar to helicopter parents are *concierge parents,* parents who believe they have to provide their kids with whatever they want. These parents have a need to make their kids' lives comfortable because their own comfort depends on it. The pain of seeing their children struggle or be in pain is more than they can bear. Another characteristic that contributes to addiction is emotional hypersensitivity, an inability to tolerate uncomfortable, painful feelings. Distressing emotions, such as anxiety, fear, anger, guilt, sadness, and depression, are often experienced as overwhelming, almost suffocating.

The use of substances and other manifestations of addiction becomes a way to turn down the volume of such feelings. Avoiding the upset of seeing one's children in distress by making certain they have whatever they want serves the same purpose. In recovery, you learn that feelings are not facts and will pass. Through mindfulness, you can develop the skills of distress tolerance and emotional regulation.

Similar to one of the hallmarks of codependency—a pattern of doing for someone else what he or she needs do for him- or herself—helicopter and concierge parenting is evident when parents do *developmentally inappropriate* things for their children. By developmentally inappropriate, I mean the child can and should be doing it (whatever *it* is) for him- or herself, whether it's tying a third-grader's shoes, selecting a sixth-grader's clothing for school, doing a tenth-grader's homework, or writing a paper for a college student.

Parental overinvolvement undermines children's growth and development by encouraging and enabling them to underfunction. It robs kids of important challenges and problem-solving experiences that provide essential opportunities to test and refine their real-world problem-solving skills, to feel and work through emotional pain, and to expand their resiliency.

Many parents don't comprehend that overprotection is embedded in all forms of overparenting, and overprotection is a subtle but unmistakable form of rejection. The overprotection inherent in doing for one's children what they can and should be doing for themselves communicates, "I don't believe you are capable of doing this yourself," or "I don't trust you to be able to do it," or "I don't think you have the competence to do it on your own." The corollary message is "If I thought/believed/trusted that you could do it, I would have allowed/encouraged/insisted that you do it yourself." Now, this all takes place unconsciously, and parents certainly don't intend it as a rejection, but think how devastating this is to a child. They may not be consciously aware of this message, but children hear it nonetheless, and it resonates deep within. Consider the damage it can do to a child's developing sense of self.

Kids grow strong wings when parents provide assistance—materially and emotionally—in ways and under conditions that support rather than weaken their kids' sense of personal responsibility and accountability. Providing help to our kids as they move into adulthood is most effective when:

- it is responsive to their current real-life circumstances;
- it balances their need for assistance with their need for autonomy;

- we provide only as much help as they legitimately need from us;

- it complements rather than replaces their own efforts.

Past a certain point in development, in order for their kids to move forward, parents need to step back. It's similar to the process of planting very young trees: The fragility of young, newly planted trees often necessitates support using stakes and ties until the trees are strong enough to continue growing without them. The stakes need to be secure but not too tight, and the ties firm enough to hold the tree upright and minimize injury to the trunk, yet flexible enough to allow room for the tree to sway in the wind. The support stakes and ties are used only long enough for the tree to become securely established and capable of standing on its own. At a certain point in its development, the tree grows beyond the need for these supports, and their continuing use can inhibit its growth. Once the supports have served their purpose, we must leave the tree to its own resources to withstand heavy winds and weather. Standing on its own, it will acquire greater strength and resiliency and be able to negotiate ever more significant challenges.

Recovery is also a process of developing roots then wings. It means experiencing and mourning the loss of parts of our lives and ourselves that we have grown beyond, which no longer serve our learning, growth, and healing. In the same ways that our recovery and our approach to it evolve over time, so should our parenting.

The experience of recovery differs at six months clean than at two years, at five years than at ten, and so on. And the same holds true with regard to parenting. The needs and capacities of our children and our approach to meeting those needs must change as they grow and move through different stages of development, each of which has somewhat different challenges—for them and for us.

3

GROWING BEYOND
HOW YOU GREW UP

*It's a far-gone lullaby
sung many years ago,
Mama, Mama, many worlds I've come
since I first left home.*

Robert Hunter, "Brokedown Palace," Grateful Dead

Nature (our genetics) and nurture (our upbringing and environment) combine to make us who we are, along with our past experiences, especially during childhood, become legacies that leave lasting imprints. The messages received from our family of origin influence how we learn to relate to ourselves, to others, and to the world. The reality of human emotional life is that our parents or other primary caregivers—and the quality of our relationships with them—loom large in our lives long after we have moved away, casting massive shadows and begetting psychological echoes that reverberate throughout our lives.

Regardless of what we present to the outside world, every family has challenges, its own special blend of wounds (sometimes going back generations) that manifest in dysfunction ranging from nightmarish abuse to normative hurts that can still cut deep and leave noticeable scars. While some families seem much healthier than others, so-called "normal" families are families we just don't know that well.

Many, though certainly not all, parents in recovery come from family systems with uncommon levels of anxiety-provoking stress-inducing dysfunction. They may find themselves treating their own kids the way they were treated as children, teenagers, or young adults. Or they may engage in overcompensation for the harsh criticism, rejection, or lack of interest they experienced from their parents by being overly permissive, having fewer limits and expectations, or more porous boundaries with their own kids. Wracked with guilt about how their active addiction affected their children, many parents compensate (or overcompensate, as the case may be) by overindulging them. They may treat their children like adults, perhaps relying on them as confidantes, or give them age-inappropriate responsibilities related to taking care of the household or younger siblings. They may be overprotective and overinvolved, envision themselves more as a friend than a parent, or confuse these often contradictory roles.

How parents were themselves parented ineluctably affects their own parenting. As Virginia Satir, a social worker and author who is considered to be the mother of Family System Therapy, expressed it: "What lingers from the parent's individual past, unresolved or incomplete, often becomes part of her or his irrational parenting." However, as you know from recovery, whatever happened to you in the past doesn't have the final say in who you are or what you become. Likewise, how you were parented need not define the kind of parent you will be.

A Different Kind of Attachment

Roots and Wings references two different conceptions of attachment. As noted in the previous chapter, the Buddhist perspective views attachment as unhealthy, out-of-balance desire for or clinging to something or someone. In contrast, *attachment theory* relates to how our early experiences with our parents or other primary caregivers—the quality of our early "attachments"—shape who we are and how we behave as adults. Originated by British psychiatrist and psychoanalyst John Bowlby and expanded by American developmental psychologist Mary Ainsworth, attachment theory is increasingly used to explain how people function in relationships and how their capacity to function in relationships, including parenting, can be upgraded.

Through early childhood experiences with parents or other primary caregivers, young children learn lifelong lessons about emotion and connection, and develop an enduring template of how relationships work. We store this information deep in the memory recesses outside conscious awareness and carry it into adulthood, influencing our later relationships with significant others—most notably intimate partners and children.

Because young children are so completely dependent upon their primary caregivers to take care of their survival needs, maintaining a secure attachment with those caregivers is an evolutionary necessity. A *secure attachment* means that when a child is distressed, a primary caregiver is physically and emotionally available to help provide comfort, and the child knows this. A secure attachment is a function of parents being attuned, responsive, and engaged *enough* with their children. As mentioned before, children require such an attachment to grow strong, healthy roots; secure attachment creates a sense of basic trust in the world as a safe place.

The emotional development of young children depends on their parents' capacity to help them tolerate and regulate their feelings. When parents are able to be present, understanding, and compassionate in the face of their children's expression of emotion, particularly when the feelings are intense or overwhelming, children experience a sense of safety and security. This helps to calm their nervous system and turns down the volume of felt emotion, effectively regulating it. Children learn that their emotions are okay. They learn that it's not only safe but also helpful to feel and to express them.

When parents are attuned and accepting of the full range of their children's feelings (and the feelings their children's emotional expression bring up for them) it strengthens healthy attachment and contributes powerfully toward self-acceptance, the essence of the quality holding environment. The more different kinds of feelings we learn how to manage as children, the more complete and healthy our emotional life will be as we progress through each stage of development into adulthood. We are then equipped to bring this emotional openness into our relationships with our intimate partners and our children.

No matter how good our parenting skills may be, at times all parents are anxious, impatient, frustrated, distracted, or irritated, and our initial reaction to our children's emotional expression is unattuned and insensitive. If, however, as parents we are mindful, exercise conscious awareness to recognize our unhelpful response, and take responsibility for it—by making amends, Tenth Step-style—whatever momentary harm was done is quickly repaired and an empathic connection is established.

Whenever you can navigate these sorts of glitches, acknowledging and correcting them, it deepens healthy attachment with your children. Their sense of security is actually strengthened by experiences that your connection with them is durable enough to withstand challenges and setbacks. Helping your children build healthy and secure attachments is not about being a perfect parent; it's about bringing conscious awareness to bear when communication with them goes awry and making the efforts needed to repair the tears in the fabric of connection.

Unfortunately, many parents and other primary caregivers lack this level of awareness and cannot tolerate their own emotions, much less those of their children. Their children then grow up with less attuned parents. An extensive meta-analysis of previous scientific studies that included nearly 2,000 children in eight countries indicated that 40 to 50 percent of very young children had insecure attachments because their caregivers were distracted, dismissive, unreliable, absent, self-absorbed, overbearing, or even threatening.[10]

Even before children develop the ability to talk, they begin to sense which feelings make their parents comfortable and bring them close and which ones cause distress and result in their parents pulling away. Over time and experience, kids develop an intuitive understanding that certain emotions are safe to feel and express while others are not. Unconsciously, they make adjustments in how they interact with their parents, learning to express the emotions that keep their parents connected with them and suppress those that jeopardize that connection.

When parents repeatedly express impatience or irritation when their children are fearful, anxiety or anger when their children feel hurt, or criticism or dismissiveness when their children are angry, an unmistakable message is received. Perhaps the most dismissive and invalidating thing a parent can say to a child in response to an expression of emotion is "You shouldn't feel that way," and yet it's all too common. Children's interpretation of such experiences is that parts of themselves are "bad" and must be hidden.

The emotions that generate such parental reactions become interwoven with a sense of danger, creating anxiety that activates the sympathetic division of the autonomic nervous system within the central nervous system, and triggers children's fight-flight-freeze stress response. Emotions perceived as unsafe are suppressed, narrowing the range of children's emotional expression. The feedback children receive through their parents' reactions as to which emotions are okay and which aren't gets wired into their brain circuitry, and the more these patterns of interaction repeat, the more defined the related neural pathways become.

10   Marinus H. Van IJzendoorn and Pieter M. Kroonenberg, "Cross-Cultural Patterns of Attachment: A Meta-Analysis of the Strange Situation," *Child Development* 59, no. 1 (February 1988): 147–156.

The unconsciously encoded strategy to express and even amplify some emotions and erase others is adaptive insofar as it facilitates connection to life-sustaining caregiving, but it comes with the brutal trade-off of compromising the ability to feel and share emotions of vulnerability, which continues across different stages of development. Whereas when children are young this schema serves a self-protective purpose, it long outlives its usefulness, later manifesting as an automatic default reaction whenever they perceive—however unconsciously—a potential threat to their basic emotional safety.

These children grow into adults with just-below-the-surface, hair-trigger stress responses and on-guard patterns of relating to others, focused on avoiding the possibility of rejection and abandonment. Having become cut off from the ability to feel and express the full range of their emotions, the capacity to negotiate the emotional decathlon requisite for real human intimacy is sacrificed on the altar of self-protection. Consequently, their relationships with partners, children, and themselves suffer.

Fortunately, history is not destiny. There are actions people can take and skills they can learn and practice to enhance their capacity for healthy relationships, including with their children. Even in adulthood, it's possible to have emotionally corrective experiences and form secure attachments that override outdated, flawed blueprints of interpersonal connection and intimacy internalized in early childhood. Both twelve-step recovery and mindfulness practices provide such experiences.

People with histories of unhealthy, insecure attachments become more emotionally secure when they form close relationships with more emotionally secure people. Those in twelve-step recovery will notice that this describes an important aspect of establishing and maintaining a relationship with a sponsor. It also speaks to why members need to be selective in choosing a sponsor.

Moreover, twelve-step programs have the capacity to provide attuned and responsive holding environments by creating a space where people can feel safe enough to allow themselves to become vulnerable, speaking openly about the most sensitive aspects of their lives, where they can feel heard and understood at depth and be accepted in ways that encourage learning and growth and promote self-acceptance. Many of us in twelve-step recovery have had the experience that pain shared is pain lessened, and joy shared is joy multiplied. This is "the therapeutic value of one addict helping another."

The mindfulness practice of intentional breathing (detailed in Chapter Six) can help parents better regulate their emotions by helping to calm emotional intensity. Tuning in to your breathing by bringing your attention to the present-moment sensation of your inhale and exhale and consciously making your breathing slower and deeper decreases pulse rate and blood pressure, reduces stress, and activates the body's relaxation response by engaging the parasympathetic division of the autonomic nervous system.

Through a variety of mindfulness practices, parents can dramatically shift their relationship to their own feelings. You can expand your emotional capacity, growing beyond the self-imposed limitations you learned so long ago in galaxies far away, and develop the ability to observe and be nonjudgmentally present with the full continuum of emotion. When you can tolerate and accept your own feelings, you can be more attuned and responsive to those of your children, your partner, and others.

Trauma Is More Common than You Think

Trauma is a Greek word meaning "wound." It's a mind-body reaction that occurs in response to events perceived as threating to one's physical and/or psychological security. Basically, trauma results from experiences stressful enough to disrupt a person's sense of safety and security and leads to feelings of helplessness and extreme vulnerability.

Although traumatic experiences often involve a threat to life or safety, any situation that leaves you feeling overwhelmed and alone can be traumatic, even if it doesn't involve physical harm.

Such experiences overload an individual's ability to cope with the emotions, sensations, and other information connected with them.

Trauma may involve a single brief event, an event that lasts for hours or days, a series of events, or an ongoing situation. Traumatic events can be directly experienced, witnessed, learned from others, or seen and read about in news reports. In general, the closer to the event someone is, the more traumatized he or she is likely to be. In other words, those who experience the event directly are more likely to be traumatized than those who witnessed or learned about it, and those who witnessed the event are more likely to be traumatized than those who learned about it indirectly. The more severe an event is and the longer it lasts, the more likely it is to be traumatizing as well.

It isn't the objective facts about an event that determine whether it's traumatic, but rather someone's subjective emotional experience of it. What is traumatic for someone else might not be for you and vice versa. How people respond to events varies considerably, and that response is influenced by multiple factors, including how the immediate environment responds—most importantly one's family and community. The more frightened, helpless, and alone you feel, the more likely you are to be traumatized.

Trauma can be especially harmful when it occurs during childhood because children are more vulnerable and have less capacity to understand and process their experiences. Childhood trauma can result from exposure to anything that interferes with a child's sense of safety and security. Tragically, many people experience trauma within their own families.

The Effects of Trauma

Traumatic experiences change the brain and alter certain physiological responses. Trauma switches on the sympathetic division of the autonomic nervous system, activating the fight-flight-freeze stress response, and the body's stress response gets stuck in the "on" position—like a car alarm that won't turn off—causing chronic stress. Your behavior, your outlook on the future, and your attitude and beliefs about people are all impacted by the experience of trauma. Following a traumatic event, most people experience a wide range of physical and emotional reactions. It's important to know that these are essentially normal reactions to abnormal events. The emotional and psychological symptoms of trauma include the following:

- shock, denial, or disbelief

- feeling generally unsafe

- hypervigilance—constantly "on guard"

- anger and irritability

- mood swings

- guilt, shame, self-blame

- sadness, depression, hopelessness

- distressing memories or thoughts about the event(s)

- confusion and difficulty concentrating

- difficulty trusting

- anxiety and fear

- withdrawing from others

- feeling disconnected, detached, or numb

Trauma Takes Many Forms

When we think of trauma, we usually think of horrific events such as war, acts of terrorism, natural disasters (hurricanes, tornadoes, forest fires, and earthquakes), plane or train crashes, motor vehicle accidents, or violent crimes (public shootings, murders, and physical/ sexual assaults), sometimes referred to as *Big-T traumas*. Big-T traumas that occur in families include being subjected to and/or witnessing physical or sexual abuse.

Yet, the majority of people experience a more subtle and chronic form of trauma, sometimes known as *small-t traumas*. These small-t traumas come from repetitive experiences that most often occur during childhood and adolescence.

Small-t Traumas

Small-t traumas can be any life experience that causes lasting harm to a person's sense of self and self-esteem. They are wounds to heart and spirit so common in families where the parents do the best they can, given their own limitations. Small-t traumas represent failures of attachment between parents and their children, often resulting from various forms of abandonment and rejection that children experience when their parents or primary caregivers are not physically or emotionally available in the ways they need. Name-calling, put-downs, verbal abuse, not knowing if or when a parent is coming home, or the fear that comes from listening to one's parents argue or fight night after night can be traumatic for any child. When parents place great pressure on their children to perform—whether in school, sports, or other endeavors—that ongoing stress can also have the effect of a small-t trauma.

Many of these kinds of traumas are common for people in recovery from addiction—especially those who grew up in addicted, violent, impoverished, or otherwise unstable or even unsafe family systems and neighborhoods. Parents need to be aware—related to their own experience, as well as to that of their children—that trauma can be caused by seemingly small events that continue to happen over an extended period, and small-t traumas are no less harmful than "bigger" traumas.

Because the events occur repeatedly—even if they continue to be stressful, upsetting, and painful—the affected person (most often a child) becomes used to them. When such events become part of one's ongoing life experience, they no longer stand out as unusual; they become "normal" and "just the way it is." With enough exposure, virtually anything, no matter how unhealthy or horrific, can seem normal. Though an insidious process, it is also a form of self-protection, allowing children to better bear the pain of circumstances far beyond their control.

The cumulative impacts of small-t traumas often remain hidden from those who experience them. The thoughts and feelings endure, but they haven't been emotionally processed and persist in the unconscious—outside of awareness. When these children become adults, the accumulated trauma affects their relationships (both romantic and social) with other adults and their own children. Feelings connected to such past traumatic experiences can be triggered, leading to conflict and over-the-top emotional reactions completely out of proportion to the current situation. Instead of responding consciously in the here and now, the person reacts unconsciously from the there and then.

The Relationship between Trauma and Addiction

Trauma and addiction often go hand in hand. Although addiction isn't caused by trauma, and trauma isn't caused by addiction, they regularly occur together, or co-occur.

Scientific studies indicate that the percentage of people with both trauma and addiction is at least 50 percent and perhaps as high as 80 percent. Although vulnerability to developing addiction increases with exposure to trauma, the connection between trauma and addiction is a two-way street: while trauma increases the risk of developing addiction, active addiction increases the likelihood of experiencing trauma.

Through the use of substances and other addictive behaviors, people initially experience the reward of feeling "good" and the relief of feeling "better." Alcohol and other drug use is a way to temporarily numb or escape the distressing effects of trauma. Using can take the form of self-medicating intrusive memories, distressing thoughts, and painful emotions linked to traumatic experiences. In this way, addiction can begin as a coping method and evolve into an emotional survival strategy. When alcohol or other drug use provides the relief someone seeks, this behavior becomes positively reinforced; the person progressively gravitates to it obsessively and compulsively; and through repetition over time it becomes addiction.

The obsessive-compulsive cycle of using alcohol and other drugs impairs judgment and decision-making in ways that often lead to risk-taking behaviors, potentially putting people in harm's way and greatly increasing the likelihood they will be traumatized or retraumatized (if they have been traumatized previously). And obviously, being under the influence puts people at much greater risk of being traumatized or retraumatized.

Healing from Trauma

Healing from trauma doesn't mean that life goes back to the way it once was. When the fabric of your world is torn, mending it creates a revised version of "normal." Recovery from trauma takes time and requires access to the conditions that promote healing. If an individual who has experienced trauma doesn't have access to recovery-supportive conditions, the effects of trauma may continue indefinitely. For those in recovery from addiction, this can translate to an ongoing risk for relapse. To mitigate that risk, people in recovery are well advised to consider the following courses of action.

Become familiar with emotional regulation and distress tolerance skills.
The terms "emotional regulation" and "distress tolerance" come from Dialectical Behavior Therapy (DBT). Emotional regulation is one of the positive byproducts of mindfulness practice. It relates to identifying emotions being felt in the moment and observing them without being overwhelmed by them. Basically, you allow yourself to feel what you feel when you feel it. Acknowledge your feelings about the trauma as they arise and strive to accept them without judgment.

Emotional regulation skills include self-soothing activities that provide a calming effect and help reduce emotional intensity. In addition to mindfulness practices and meditation (detailed in Chapters Five and Six), relaxation and stress reduction practices such as listening to music you enjoy, taking a walk, reading something pleasurable or spiritual, singing a favorite song, exercising, visualizing a comforting or relaxing image, and journaling can all help. Emotional regulation involves learning how to modulate your feelings. When you can turn down the intensity of your feelings, your capacity to be aware of and manage your impulses increases and you are less likely to act in reactive, self-defeating, and destructive ways.

Distress tolerance means learning how to be okay with uncomfortable emotions and difficult sensations, enduring and accepting discomfort, and learning to bear pain skillfully. Distress tolerance skills grow from mindfulness practices and involve the ability to nonjudgmentally accept both yourself and the current situation in spite of whatever emotional and physical discomfort you experience. Remember, acceptance does not equal approval. You can learn to tolerate thoughts, emotions, physical sensations, and situations that you don't like at all and may even deeply dislike. Distress tolerance enhances coping capacity by strengthening resiliency—the ability to adjust to change.

Minimize isolation by connecting with others and *seeking out support.*
It's important to talk about your thoughts and feelings and ask for the help you need. The twelve-step programs of recovery are among the most therapeutic sources of support available. If you're already a member of a twelve-step program, you may find it helpful to increase your involvement by attending more meetings, speaking with your sponsor more frequently, and making greater use of your twelve-step support system. If you don't participate in a twelve-step program of recovery, now may be an excellent time to connect with one or use other supportive resources to which you have access: a trusted family member, friend, counselor, or clergy. Support from family and friends can have a hugely positive impact on coping with trauma.

Participate in social activities, even if you don't feel like it

Consider volunteering. As well as helping others, volunteering helps you reconnect with people and mitigates the sense of helplessness that often accompanies trauma. Being of service by helping others in your family, neighborhood, community, or twelve-step program takes the focus off yourself while serving as a reminder of your abilities and strengths. It also helps you reclaim a sense of competence and self-efficacy.

Practice self-compassion

Compassion means recognizing the pain of others and experiencing a desire to help to reduce their suffering (offering understanding and kindness to others when they struggle, make mistakes, or fail, for example). Self-compassion turns that same response toward yourself. Instead of harshly judging and criticizing yourself for your inadequacies, you try to be kind and understanding with yourself. Having compassion for yourself means honoring your humanness by accepting yourself when you struggle with challenges—including the effects of traumatic experiences—and fall short of your ideals. (Self-compassion is detailed further in Chapter Six.)

Seek out professional trauma treatment as needed.

Healing trauma frequently benefits from professional treatment, especially if the trauma is or was severe, complex, or repetitive. The ultimate purposes of treatment are to help free the individual from the grip of the effects of trauma and begin to live in the present with an enhanced sense of safety, competence, and personal responsibility. (Recovering from trauma that has progressed to Post-Traumatic Stress Disorder (PTSD) generally requires professional assistance.)

There are currently three primary trauma treatment modalities. In *exposure therapy*, people reexperience and talk through the traumatic event through guided exercises designed to maximize emotional safety, over and over, until the event no longer activates trauma reactions. *Eye Movement Desensitization and Reprocessing (EMDR)* involves several techniques to help people reexamine, reprocess, and integrate traumatic memories and events. *Somatic therapies*—the most notable of which are Somatic Experiencing and Sensorimotor Psychotherapy—emphasize the use of the body to process trauma and facilitate the integration of traumatic memories and experiences.

Change Is a Motherf'er

Most people have a hard time accepting the need to change and find it even harder to actually make meaningful life changes. Let's face it, change is scary. There is a natural fear of the unknown and the uncertainty that comes with it. It takes strength and courage to do anything different or unfamiliar because unfamiliarity breeds discomfort, and the more unfamiliar "it" is, the more discomfort we feel. Importantly, courage is not the absence of fear. Courage is acknowledging your fear and doing what you need to do in spite of it.

It's not unusual for people to stay in painful, unhealthy situations, sometimes for years, even when they know they need to make changes. Because they are familiar with the pain of their specific situation—they know exactly how it works and what the results will be—there is a certain predictability and comfort in it. Most people become motivated to make major life changes only when the pain of staying the same outweighs the fear of doing something different. Those of us in recovery from addiction know well how this dynamic works.

The process of making significant changes in any area of life unfolds over time and involves progressing through a series of stages, detailed in the Transtheoretical Model of Change. This model can be applied to a wide range of behaviors and life areas—including addiction and recovery—and while the amount of time a person spends in each stage varies, the order of stages does not change.

The Transtheoretical Model of Change

Developed by psychologists James O. Prochaska and Carlo C. DiClemente, this model integrates multiple theories about the process of change and boils them down to five straightforward stages.

1. Precontemplation/Not Yet Ready/Not Thinking about Change

People are unaware their behavior is problematic, contributes to problems, or creates negative consequences. They see no reason to consider changing or making improvements.

2. Contemplation/Getting Ready

People think about the possibility of making changes. They have an awareness of a problem that requires change or improvement, but they're either not yet ready to do anything about it or uncertain what to do about it. Ambivalence about whether to make changes in the first place, as well as what changes to make and how to go about making them, can cause people to remain in this stage for long periods of time.

3. Preparation/Readiness

People understand that behavioral change is necessary and are ready to take action. They begin to take small steps toward making improvements in their behavior.

4. Action

People make concerted changes and improvements in their behavior—by modifying their existing behaviors, acquiring new healthier behaviors, or both. Action is observable and can include starting treatment or counseling voluntarily, discontinuing the use of alcohol and other drugs, actively engaging in the process of recovery by attending twelve-step meetings and getting a sponsor, beginning to meditate or making meditation a consistent daily practice, engaging in other mindfulness practices, eating healthier, and exercising regularly.

5. Maintenance

People have been able to sustain healthy changes and are committed to continuing and further building upon them going forward. Maintenance is the stage in which people work to prevent relapse into past unhelpful and unhealthy behaviors.

If you're reading this, you're most likely in the stage of Contemplation, Readiness, or Action, based on your interest in developing your parenting knowledge and skills. However, some readers may be in the Maintenance stage and interested in enriching their current parenting knowledge and skills.

Principles of Behavior Change

There are certain dynamics that are universal to all forms of behavior change.

- Change is a messy process of trial, error, and experimentation.

- Change involves taking risks.

- Mistakes are opportunities to learn and adjust.

- Change includes "failure." (Actually, there is no such thing as failure, only information. Even when attempts at change don't yield the desired outcome(s), they provide valuable information that can be integrated into future attempts at change and, therefore, are successes.)

- Change often feels worse before it feels better.

- Small pebbles can make big ripples—small-scale changes can reverberate widely and have unforeseen potency.

Awareness and Action

In order to be successful in any process of meaningful change, both awareness and action are necessary. Without awareness of your current status (where you are now) and your goals (where you want to be), your actions will lack direction and effectiveness, wasting precious time and energy. So awareness is important, but awareness by itself rarely results in change—only doing things differently leads to change.

To succeed in and sustain any process of significant change, whether in recovery or in parenthood, we require both awareness and action. Translating conscious awareness into intentional action in parenting parallels the process of learning and developing new skills in any area of life, be it sports, cooking, auto repair, reading, gardening, painting, plumbing, or meditating. In order to get better at anything, we need to

1. learn specifically what works;

2. practice what works with persistence and dedication, even (or perhaps especially) when it seems really hard or we don't feel like it.

The Four Stages of Learning and Skill Development

Milton Erickson (no relation to Erik) was a psychiatrist and psychotherapist who had an extraordinary grasp of human perception and behavior with an emphasis on unconscious processes. He believed that each and every person is inherently competent and has all the internal resources necessary to make the changes they seek. His approach to clinical hypnotherapy brought light-year advances to that method of helping people make positive, healthy change, and his work was instrumental to the development of brief forms of psychotherapy, as well as solution-focused therapy and Neuro-Linguistic Programming (NLP).

According to Erickson, the process of learning and skill development in any area has four stages: unconscious incompetence, conscious incompetence, conscious competence, and unconscious competence.

Unconscious incompetence is a state of obliviousness—not knowing something but also not knowing that you don't know it, and therefore not caring about it one way or another. Similar to the precontemplation stage of change, being unconsciously incompetent, in terms of parenting, means that parents have no awareness of their parenting as problematic and unskillful, and in turn, no interest in even considering doing anything differently.

At the point of recognizing their parenting approach does not work well and contributes to distress for both their children and themselves, parents progress to *conscious incompetence.* They become consciously aware of the potential value of making changes in how they parent and may have an understanding of what they want or need to do differently. They begin to make positive, healthy changes in their parenting but struggle in their efforts, which they know are often awkward and unskillful.

Through persistent practice and experience, they gradually achieve *conscious competence,* building the knowledge and skills to implement their desired improvements proficiently and consistently. Conscious competence reflects the ability to do something well or skillfully. However, the action requires thinking intentionally about each aspect of it. For instance, when my daughters express emotional pain, it still precipitates distress for me, and I experience an immediate and automatic wish/need/impulse to try to "fix" or take away their pain. I have to be consciously aware of my internal reactions and be present with my own pain in order to be present with theirs. Then I can take deliberate care in finding the words most likely to be attuned and helpful. This is an example of mindfulness in action.

Unconscious competence is also known as mastery. When athletes describe being "in the zone," they are in a state of unconscious competence. They perform at such a high level as to seem unstoppable. Yet, every aspect of their performance appears effortless, almost as if they're operating on autopilot, in sync with the universe. They don't have to think about what to do, it just happens.

The more present-centered and mindful I am, the more intentionally I can act; the more I have the capacity to choose how I wish to respond to specific circumstances in any area of life, including parenting and recovery. Riding a bike, reading, swimming, playing sports, keyboarding/typing, and playing video games are examples of everyday activities that all progress through Erickson's four stages of learning—improving with enough practice and repetition to become unconscious and automatic.

As challenging as it can be to learn and develop new skills in any area, in comparison to recovery and parenting, the above examples are simple and concrete. Skills such as accepting things you really want to change but can't, observing your thoughts, maintaining present-moment awareness, communicating in ways both supportive and responsive, and coexisting with distressing emotions without pushing them away or acting on them in ways that make situations worse are incredibly difficult skills to master.

Skillful parenting requires a high degree of moment-to-moment, conscious attention and awareness, especially in emotionally charged, heat-of-the-moment situations. As a result, unconscious competence in parenting may be unrealistic, but more importantly, it may be unnecessary because mindful parenting is the real goal.

Once you have learned a skill well enough to successfully apply it in action, it becomes a resource you can use in a broad assortment of circumstances. In other words, once you have learned how to read, it doesn't matter whether the length of a book is forty pages or four hundred pages; once you know how to swim, you can swim in water that's five feet deep or five hundred feet deep. The terrain may be quite different, but the application of learning and skill remains fundamentally the same. The same dynamic applies to parenting knowledge and skills.

Experience Changes the Brain

Neuroscience demonstrates that the human brain has the ability to change and adapt throughout a person's life. This ability, known as *neuroplasticity*, allows the brain's structure and functioning to change in response to new knowledge and experiences (internal, interactional, and external). In this process, our brains do not distinguish between good and bad, healthy and unhealthy. Our brains learn and shift in response to whatever is repeated—thought patterns, how we relate to our emotions, and behaviors.

Neurons are cells within the brain and nervous system that transmit information to other nerves, muscles, and glands. Glands release hormones such as oxytocin and cortisol (the "stress hormone," which increases heart rate, blood pressure, arousal, and anxiety). Through new information, experiences, and actions, the brain continuously lays down new neural pathways to process and communicate information. When you repeat an experience over and over, the brain learns to trigger the same neurons each time, and the connection between them (the specific neural pathway) becomes stronger, thus the phrase "neurons that fire together wire together." Conversely, unused or rarely used neural connections weaken.

The brain adapts to repetitive experiences by strengthening the relevant neural pathways, basically forming memory tracks that work in the brain's operating system, outside conscious awareness. When repeated consistently over time, any activity, behavior, or experience—whether healthy and positive or unhealthy and destructive—creates new unconscious memory tracks.

When neurons communicate frequently, messages that repeatedly travel the same pathway in the brain begin to transmit faster and more efficiently, not unlike grading, paving, and widening a roadway to allow traffic to travel more easily and efficiently. Over time, enough repetition of an experience or activity can turn a one-lane road into an interstate freeway.

The brain changes both physically and functionally as connections between neurons are generated, rewired, and refined. The brain's capacity to make these changes gives us the ability to memorize new facts, form new memories, adjust to new experiences and environments, integrate new learning, and develop new skills. The memory tracks created through repetitive experiences serve to deepen learning and strengthen mental, emotional, and muscle memory.

The formation of these memory tracks eventually allows activities to be performed without conscious thought or effort. With enough repetition, they become automatic, and habits are born. For example, repetitive substance use, along with its related activities and behaviors, creates new neural pathways and unconscious memory tracks. For most people in active addiction, the experience of pain—whether physical or emotional—follows an established neural pathway or memory track (a six-lane freeway) and translates instantly into a desire to use. These memory tracks manifest in the literal habits of one's addiction—the patterns, routines, and rituals that accompany and reinforce thinking, feeling, and acting in ways that continue to fuel using.

In recovery, the brain has the opportunity to heal and rebuild the connections damaged and distorted during active addiction. Consistent with neuroplasticity, the brain is extremely resilient and can adapt to new and different repetitive experiences. That's what gives us older dogs the capacity to learn and master new tricks. Each day we have the opportunity to strengthen the neural pathways that support recovery. Similarly, through new or modified ways of thinking and acting with regard to how you parent, including learning mindfulness-related approaches and skills, you can create new neural pathways. With repetition, the neural connections that support attuned, empathic, and responsive parenting become stronger, more durable, and more efficient.

Expanding Feelings of Kindness, Appreciation, Compassion, and Love

Depending upon the family in which you were raised, the messages you received growing up, and the makeup of your personality, emotions such as kindness, appreciation, compassion, and love may or may not come naturally to you. Fortunately, these emotions correlate directly with certain actions and can be developed with intention and attention so that you can bring them into your interactions with others—most importantly your children.

Practicing such actions constructs and fortifies neural pathways associated with these emotions. Like water and fertilizer on a newly planted garden, these actions help cultivate kindness, appreciation, compassion, and love so they bloom more fully and we feel them more deeply. To draw further on John Bruna's exquisite metaphor, our attention is like water: whatever we water grows larger, so we can choose to water the flowers rather than the weeds of our thoughts and emotions by tuning in to feelings of kindness, appreciation, compassion, and love by bringing them to mind, and paying attention to actions that expand our conscious contact with them.

This can begin with seemingly tiny practices like sharing a smile, extending a few kindhearted words, and being emotionally present with those we interact with—especially our children. These simple yet precious practices soften the heart and, to borrow a term from boxing, punch way above their weight. They don't cost anything extra, and we can do them even when we're having a shitty day.

Smile—intentionally and often—and smile at and with your children with regularity. A smile opens the door to kindness. A genuine smile is a small yet profound act of generosity. Besides emanating kindness and connection, smiling elevates mood by triggering the release of the feel-good neurotransmitters serotonin and dopamine. Smiling is also at least a little bit contagious; when we smile at others, it frequently elicits a smile in return. Keep in mind that, as Aesop, the ancient Greek storyteller, put it, "No act of kindness, no matter how small, is ever wasted."

Greet people when you encounter them. Say "hello," "good morning," and "good afternoon." (This is no less important to do with your children.) Even a nod of the head is an act of kindness, an acknowledgment of the other person. Whenever possible, greet people by name. Being called by one's name is among the most understated, yet powerfully validating experiences a person can have. It symbolizes recognition and connection—that you care enough about people to remember and use their names.

Say "thank you." It's a way of recognizing others and honoring their efforts. The underlying message of this easy-to-take-for-granted and frequently overlooked statement is *I see you, and we are connected.* When parents say "thank you" to their children, it both expresses appreciation and models the importance of acknowledging the kindness of others, the work they do, or the service they provide.

Engage in hugging and other forms of caring touch, such as placing an arm around someone in a show of kindness or putting a hand on another's shoulder to communicate support. Caring touch has multiple physiological and emotional benefits for both people. It reduces blood pressure, lowers cortisol, and stimulates the release of oxytocin. Touching also releases serotonin, which soothes and regulates mood. Caring touch is a primary language of childhood. It provides emotional nourishment, awakening and increasing feelings of calmness, trust, and secure attachment between parents and their children.

Make time to connect with your children, regardless of how busy you are. Tell them that you love them—often. Too many parents don't do this or only do it rarely, many assuming "they already know I love them."

One of the ironies of human nature is that all too frequently, people make an effort to be more overtly kind and considerate to other people (sometimes complete strangers) than to their own families. They may be much harder on those with whom they are closest—partners and children in particular. This was the case with my own father, and there were times I succumbed to this phenomenon as well.

For five years during the mid-1990s, I was the clinical director for a hospital-based addiction treatment program that provided medically managed detoxification and rehabilitation for adults. In addition to supervising the program's social workers and counselors, my role included functioning as a sort of vice principal, dealing directly with violations of program rules and determining consequences. We worked with an extremely challenged and challenging population, and when patients acted out—which occurred in all manner of ways—they had to meet with me. With surprising frequency, they would ask me, "Do you ever get angry?" In response, I'd smile and assure them that since anger is a natural human emotion, everyone gets angry sometimes.

On my return home, I'd tell my kids that the patients at work once again asked if I ever got angry, to which my elder daughter's reaction was a combination snort-snigger followed by an always incredulous variation on the theme of "If they only knew." While I took considerable pride in my professional self-discipline, its incongruity with the liberties of laxity I sometimes took as a parent only inspired self-reproach.

We need to be consciously aware of the tendency to take the people we love and their presence in our lives for granted and treat them less well. With this awareness, we are more likely to treat them with the kindness, appreciation, compassion, and love they deserve.

Parenting is a link in the chain that connects the past with the future. How did the way your parents talked to you influence your inner voice, your self-talk? Keep in mind that how you talk to your children becomes part of how they talk to themselves.

Every day, you participate in myriad encounters, each of which has an impact on other people, your environment, and you. The impacts of your actions ripple far beyond what you know or can observe, so with conscious effort, you can build more kindness, appreciation, compassion, and love into your actions throughout the day. The size of the actions matters not; they all have meaning and value. Everything you do that is positive makes a positive difference somehow, somewhere, and in some way, especially with your children. As expressed so elegantly by psychologist and philosopher William James, "Let everything you do be done as if it makes a difference. It does."

4

OUR CHILDREN ARE NOT US

*You may give them your love
but not your thoughts,
For they have their own thoughts.*

Kahlil Gibran, *On Children*

More than any other form of relationship, parenting muddles the lines of demarcation between self and other. Many parents are emotionally invested in their children being a certain way. Sometimes, they get caught up in how their children differ from the children they imagined or hoped they'd have. They are attached to an image of how they want their children to be, a model that often diverges from who their children are. We can become attached to the belief that our kids should be a certain way, behave in certain ways, do certain things or participate in certain activities, and perform at certain levels.

While children usually manifest some of their parents' physical and personality traits, rarely are they a full-on "mini-me."

Accepting them as they are, with all their individual differences and idiosyncrasies, promotes the growth of their roots. Honoring their needs and preferences distinct from your own nurtures the development of their wings.

Us and Them

Parents face an intriguing challenge when the interests of their children diverge significantly from their own—particularly when parents are passionate about those interests. For instance, I have always been an athlete. At an early age, I committed to putting in the time and effort to develop my skills in baseball, football, lacrosse, and basketball. I wanted to master those skills to the maximum extent of my abilities and to expand my abilities as much as I could. I practiced my ass off: with organized teams, friends, and my father (some of the most positive time we ever spent together), and by myself. Participating in organized competitive team sports during my childhood and adolescence gifted me with some of the most affirming experiences and important life lessons I've ever had. Of course, I wanted my children to experience the same benefits, but I also wanted to see them excel in this arena as I had once upon a time.

Around the age of five my elder daughter became interested in gymnastics. She had obvious talent, quickly developing a flawless one-handed cartwheel and soon attended a more rigorous training program, followed by another higher-level program. By third grade, her interest and commitment began to wane, and soon thereafter she informed her mother and me that she no longer wished to continue.

The choice was hers—and hers alone.

At about the same age she discovered gymnastics, she also started to play organized T-ball. She clearly enjoyed it and liked to practice but only up to a point. Skill development was attractive to her but not engrossing, as it had been for me. There was, however, one aspect of her skill set that stood out prominently: her throwing mechanics. By the time she was eight or nine, she demonstrated a picture-perfect overhand throwing motion that resulted in arm strength far beyond her physical stature. Her throwing mechanics—whether of a baseball, softball, or football— were immaculate from start to finish (much more than mine ever were) and culminated in a consistently precise and powerful throw. It was such a thing of beauty that I enjoyed the hell out of just watching it. (It still brings me great joy whenever we get to play catch together, in part because I get to bear witness to the artistry of her throws.) She ended up playing organized softball through eighth grade and decided she was done.

My younger daughter had less interest in sports but played T-ball and softball for a few years then basketball in middle school for a season before deciding that organized sports simply weren't for her.

Early on, I knew their interest had to be self-generated. It didn't matter how much I wanted them to participate and be successful— they had to want it and want it enough to do the necessary work. It was about *their* interests, rather than *mine*, or what I believed was in their best interests. I was committed to encouraging and supporting my daughters' interests, and I had to work to remain consciously aware of where the line of demarcation between my needs and interests and theirs fell. I was determined not to become one of those asshole parents whose kids' participation and performance was really about themselves. Too frequently, parents get ensnared in believing their children's success depends on their direction and their children's interests—as well as their misbehaviors, problems, and "failures"— are a reflection of them. This invariably creates suffering for both parents and children.

I wanted to push my kids to become better in sports but only to the extent that they wanted to. Once they no longer had the desire, it was up to me to be okay with their choices and, by extension, with them. It was a loss I needed to acknowledge to myself, absorb, mourn, and move through.

When I had nine months in recovery, my daughters' mother and I decided to separate, and shortly thereafter I moved out. It was an emotionally fraught, pain-fueled, and stress-filled time for all of us, and none of us knew how to be. But it was hardest on our younger daughter, who was fifteen and had recently started high school—as if that time of life and the bio-psycho-social development that goes with it isn't tumultuous enough.

Until I moved to Vegas a little over a year later, I'd get together with her several times each week. We spent many hours watching Japanese anime. At the time, I had no familiarity with anime and no interest in learning about it or watching it. But my daughter was enamored with the genre, and my priority was to spend time with her, minimize the further fraying of our relationship, and cushion the blows to her world. Anime was important to her; therefore, it became important to me.

We went through a number of her favorite anime series. It evolved into a bonding experience wherein, in addition to being present and watching together, I had her educate me about anime, taking a one-down position in which she was the expert. This brought us closer and turned into an unexpectedly meaningful experience for me. I learned much more about anime than I would have ever thought possible, including that I could really enjoy it. I also learned anime addresses a litany of sociocultural and humanistic issues and my daughter could speak to those issues with an eloquence and understanding far beyond her age.

Since graduating college, she works in the video game industry, refining and fine-tuning new games prior to their public release. I have no intrinsic interest in video gaming (as in none whatsoever), but I'm keenly interested in my daughter and her life, so I have become interested in video gaming. Not from the standpoint of playing, mind you, but from the perspective of having her school me, based on the projects she's working on. And, as with anime, I've learned more about video games than I would ever have anticipated, and I've enjoyed it. To be with my daughter as she explains these games and her work on them with eye-opening precision and sophistication makes my heart smile wide.

Until she went away to college, my younger daughter didn't have much interest in physical fitness. Suddenly, she turned into a workout buff, and we began hiking together during her visits.

Believe it or not, there are world-class hiking areas just outside Las Vegas, our favorite of which is the Mount Charleston wilderness in the Humboldt-Toiyabe National Forest. Depending on the trail, we hike at elevations that start between 7,500 and 8,400 feet and go up to 9,400 to 10,200 feet. We typically cover distances ranging from five to eight miles.

I adore hiking with her, although I use the term "with" loosely. During most of our first few hikes, she stayed within viewing distance but just barely. Since then, whether we hike with a group or it's just the two of us, we hike together for the first few hundred yards, after which the separation begins. As she bounds ahead on her own, the distance between her and everyone else increases, and I watch her become smaller and smaller until she disappears from my field of vision. I hike at a steady, measured pace, and she is a gazelle on the trail.

When hiking on trails that had yet to become familiar, intermittently she'd find a place to wait for me to catch up. We'd talk for a moment, and she'd be off, leaving me in the dust again. We settled into a rhythm where we began the trail together, I watched her disappear, and the next time I saw her was at an agreed-upon spot for lunch. After eating together, she quickly vanished into the forest ahead of me again, and we met back at the car. She'd get to the car about half an hour before me on average, and I started giving her the car keys at lunch so she could wait more comfortably.

As wonderful and cathartic as it was to be immersed in nature and have that experience with her, part of me really wanted to be able to spend more time with her on the trail. At the start of a hike where it was just the two of us one day, I shared that thought with her and asked if, every once in a while, she'd be willing to slow down so we could actually hike together. Her response—immediate, unequivocal, and unapologetic—cut me to the quick. "No. I want to maximize the cardio workout, and you're too slow."

My immediate internal reaction followed the sequence, *Ouch! Fuck! Really?!* Reflexively, I felt hurt and angry, but I knew from previous experience that trying to force the issue or control the situation would only create suffering for both of us on future hikes and elsewhere in life. Although her rejection and loss of the opportunity for further connection saddened me, I realized that my preference was no mandate and she was entitled to the experience that met *her* needs, which moved me toward acceptance.

Not long after that conversation, we planned a hike in a different area, a lower elevation loop trail that traversed a narrow canyon created by steep walls of sandstone and limestone. As it turned out, recent rains had flooded the canyon, and parts of the trail required negotiating three to six feet of standing water. As usual, my daughter had gone well ahead of me. She waited for me on the descent from a ridge that led down into the canyon and pointed out the obstacle giving us the middle finger.

We had two options: return to the car and leave our hike frustratingly unfinished or hike together into the canyon and help each other around and through the water. We took option number two, and I reveled in the experience of being with and assisting her step by precious step as we slowly and carefully bouldered our way across massive angled slabs of rock. I told her how happy I was that we could do the hike together, even if it was the result of extraordinary circumstances. She just smiled and nodded. While it happened only once, to this day I'm deeply grateful for it. We rarely acquire lasting contentment by getting what we want; it's found in appreciating what we have. Moreover, my gratitude to be able to share this exquisite experience of hiking with her in any form continues unabated.

Relinquishing the Need to Control

A weighty theme in twelve-step recovery is to relinquish trying to control other people and situations, to allow circumstances to unfold however they will and let life take its own course. To me, this is the crux of Step Three, but it's a challenge not unique to those in recovery. The need for control, after all, is part of being human. It's natural and normal to want certain outcomes. But, as the twelve-step saying goes, we can make plans, but we can't control outcomes.

It's healthy to have goals, and it's beneficial to plan. Problems arise, however, when we become so attached to specific outcomes that the ends justify whatever means we use, and the need to control people or situations to facilitate those outcomes steamrolls the needs and interests of others. This is a prescription for suffering— for ourselves as well as for others. And, there is a direct correlation: the more attached to an outcome you are, the greater your need for control will be, and the more suffering you are likely to cause.

Attempts to control your children in order to get an outcome you want take forms both overt (arguing, browbeating, demanding, insisting, or threatening) and indirect (manipulating, cajoling, bargaining, bribing, pleading, or guilt-tripping). My own need to control people, situations, and outcomes during my active addiction obstructed my ability to be happy—insofar as happiness was a function of contentment and peace of mind. My need to be "right" demanded a level of control that made it harder for my daughters and their mother to be happy or at peace for very long. It was a tragic source of suffering for all of us, and a wellspring for my feelings of guilt and shame.

Only when keeping conscious company with my natural inclination to control can I make an intentional choice to act according to what I believe to be most beneficial. Bringing mindfulness to bear, I can be aware of the emergence of a need to control, observe its formation, and renounce it. Without such awareness, I may well be held captive by it and act unconsciously and unskillfully.

I need to tune in where I find myself emotionally uncomfortable, in some form of dis-ease, and begin to get caught up in the need to "fix" it. As the Zen proverb suggests (a perspective shared by the Stoic philosophers of ancient Rome), *the obstacle is the path*. When I get an inkling of a need to control as it relates to my kids, coming to conscious awareness allows me to sidestep unnecessary suffering. It creates the space that makes it possible for me to experience greater contentment and enjoyment with them and be more kind, appreciative, compassionate, and loving toward them.

The importance of separating your needs and preferences from those of your children can't be overstated. Yes, they will overlap in places, and that's beautiful. However, there will be many places where they diverge, and how you deal with differences and conflicts regarding values, worldviews, interests, and priorities makes a massive difference in what happens between you and your children and what happens within your children.

Respect for the needs, interests, preferences, and decisions of your children conveys respect for them at a felt level. Accepting and honoring their needs, interests, preferences, and decisions communicates a deep acceptance of your children. Your acceptance of your children is one of the keys to their self-acceptance. This is one of the most important gifts you can give them, a gift they deserve.

Keep in mind that acceptance does not connote approval. As Norman Maclean wrote so beautifully in *A River Runs Through It and Other Stories*, "We can love completely without complete understanding." I strive to apply the wisdom of that lyrical aphorism in my relationship with my daughters. Understanding is helpful, but it is not requisite. My love for them transcends any differences or disagreements we have had or may have. I don't have to understand, agree with, or approve of all their choices or actions in order to love them completely, no matter what.

A twelve-step adage states that expectations are resentments waiting to happen. I would suggest that they are, more accurately, often disappointments in waiting. We crowd our lives with unrealistic expectations based on how we want situations and people to be, in contrast to how they are. Left unchecked, these sow the seeds of dissatisfaction and disappointment. Such expectations include that our kids should be who and how we want them to be and behave how we want them to.

In liberating us from the tyranny of active addiction and all the cover-ups that contributed to and resulted from it, recovery provides the freedom to unveil and become our true selves. Shouldn't your children also have the opportunity to be who they really are and wish to be, unchained from parental pressure and expectations to be something or someone else? Mindful parenting is about raising your children to be the best *they* can be, not the best of who you'd like them to be. Your mission is to allow our kids to be completely themselves, to nurture and support who and what *they* are.

Namaste is an ancient Sanskrit word used as a common greeting in Hindu culture and as a gesture of acknowledgment and respect in many spiritual circles, notably those relating to meditation and yoga. It means the divine in me recognizes the divine in you. Attuned, skillful parenting means recognizing, appreciating, and nurturing the divine in your children.

If I'm attached to any outcomes for my daughters, it's that they find contentment and as much happiness as possible—that's it. Still, experience continues to teach me that, ultimately, parenting is less about outcomes than it is about relationships.

Your Ex Is Not Your Children's Ex

Don't dis your ex. When a couple with children splits up, among the more emotionally damaging things either of them can do to their children is disparage the other parent in the children's presence. Children so closely identify with their parents—the younger they are, the greater their identification—that bad-mouthing the other parent in front of their children wounds them. This is another area where your needs and interests likely diverge from those of your kids. Even when the other parent has serious problems and has acted poorly to you or your children, your kids' experience of this might differ greatly from yours.

Prior to graduate school in the mid-1980s, I conducted diagnostic assessments on adolescent boys placed in temporary residential treatment due to parental neglect or abuse or their own acting out, though the two often occurred together. It never ceased to amaze me that no matter how horrifically those teens may have been abused, invariably they wanted to return home to their parents. Even in the face of grotesque mistreatment and powerfully mixed feelings, much more often than not, it seems the loyalty of children to their parents is steadfast.

You may believe that by talking shit about their other parent in front of your kids, you're helping them by revealing the "truth," but you're only causing them harm. When you denigrate their other parent, you're putting your children in a no-win position in which (consciously or unconsciously) they feel as though they have to choose between their parents. In this double-bind, they are damned if they do and damned if they don't. It's never helpful or healthy to effectively force them to choose between their parents or make them feel disloyal or "bad" for not agreeing with you or loving their other parent. Whatever legitimate complaints and criticisms you may have with reference to your children's other parent, it's essential that you keep them between you and your ex.

Holding Space

Parents who trash talk the other parent in their kids' presence have difficulty holding space for their kids. And, holding such space may well be impossible when their children's pain involves the other parent.

When you *hold space* for other people, you meet them where they are at a heart-based level, effectively walking alongside them through their experience—however challenging or distressing it may be. It conveys, "I'm right here with you." Holding space creates a safe, welcoming emotional container for the feelings and experiences of another person in which you are present with him or her, without an agenda, without judgment or giving advice, and without trying to change or fix him or her or influence the outcome.

Holding space for your children means being fully present with their experience, respecting their individual needs and differences, and accepting that they may make choices you wouldn't. Since parents are responsible for their children's safety, especially when they are younger, obviously there are many circumstances when you need to step in and make decisions for them. Parents also need to set and enforce limits and provide the structure to help their children grow strong roots. That notwithstanding, whenever possible, giving your kids the autonomy to make their own choices will serve their developmental needs best.

Skillful parents learn when to withhold guidance, for instance, when it is likely to make their children feel inadequate or incompetent. They also know when to offer it softly, as in when their children ask for it or genuinely don't know what to ask for. This balancing act takes self-awareness, humility, and practice.

To hold space for your children in ways that support their learning and growth, you have to be prepared to step aside, so they can make their own choices while at the same time providing love and support, giving gentle guidance when they ask for it or when it's truly needed, and helping them feel safe when they make mistakes. You need to hold space for them to feel safe to be themselves.

Keep in mind, you can't successfully hold space for your children (or anyone else) when they are in pain if you haven't learned how to recognize and make peace with your own pain. Parents need to learn how to take care of their own emotional needs before they can truly meet the emotional needs of their children. This self-care is consistent with the instructions airlines give to all passengers as part of the pre-takeoff safety instructions: if oxygen masks become necessary and you're traveling with a child, make sure to put on your own mask first before attempting to help your child.

In order to take appropriate care of their children, parents have to engage in appropriate self-care. Parents working a process of recovery are already engaged in self-care practices that can be added to and built upon.

When adults make a commitment to be a parent to their child, they also need to make a commitment to their own mental, emotional, physical, and spiritual health. Mindfulness and its practices can add high-octane, bio-psycho-social-spiritual fuel to help parents follow through on this commitment and expand their capacity to respond intentionally instead of automatically, better nurturing the growth and development of their children's roots and wings.

5

MIND FULL
VERSUS MINDFUL

*When mindfulness embraces those we love,
they will blossom like flowers.*

Thich Nhat Hanh

According to a notable Zen parable, a samurai known for his battlefield ferocity came to visit an esteemed Buddhist monk, demanding, "Teach me about heaven and hell. Tell me everything you know!"

To the samurai's astonishment, the monk replied contemptuously, "I will tell you nothing. You come uninvited, fail to introduce yourself, and shout demands for knowledge. You are arrogant and ignorant, and you smell like a hundred decomposing cows."

The samurai instantly flew into a rage. He drew his sword, yelling, "I could kill you for such disrespect!"

He was ready to strike when the monk calmly stated, "That is hell."

Taken aback by the monk's composed observation about the fury that had him in its grip, the samurai stopped in his tracks; his face softened. Grateful for the monk's insight and humbled by his wisdom and courage, he put down his sword and bowed.

"And that," the monk said gently, "is heaven."

The samurai's awakening to his anger and its influence over him illustrates the all-important difference between being caught up in a feeling and becoming aware that you are being swept away by it. Awareness of one's own feelings as they occur is a keystone of emotional intelligence. Many people live in the hell of being at the whims and fluctuating winds of their emotions. Applying the mindfulness practice of consciously tuning in to your emotional state and learning to separate feelings from actions is a small slice of heaven.

As parents, who among us hasn't fallen prey to a rising tide of emotion in reaction to our kids? It's not uncommon to be swamped by a wave of frustration, irritation, and anger with your kids, occasionally acting out impulsively by yelling at them. Perhaps a wave of guilt or even shame follows in close pursuit, upending you further. I've certainly been there and done that.

Mindfulness is an approach to living as well as a range of practices that emphasize paying conscious attention to the present moment by tuning in to one's internal and external experience. Mindfulness creates a receptive state in which one observes and accepts his or her thoughts, emotions, physical sensations, and interactions with others as they are, without judging or needing to change them.

Mindfulness cultivates the ability to witness one's own experience without becoming caught up in and attached to the content of thoughts, emotions, and physical sensations *or* trying to avoid or suppress them. Although meditation is one of the best-known practices to achieve a state of mindfulness, there are many others. Mindfulness has origins in Buddhism and Taoism, but it has no connection to religion. While many people use mindfulness practices, including meditation, to enhance their spirituality, many simply use these practices to find greater mental and emotional clarity and balance and to improve their overall health and well-being.

The Mind as Storyteller

On any given day, when you're brushing your teeth in the morning at home alone in your bathroom, are you really in your bathroom or are you somewhere else? And are you alone, or are other people there with you? How much of your attention is actually focused on brushing your teeth versus the anticipated events of the day ahead or something else completely unrelated to what you're doing in that moment?

How many times have you been driving and missed your intended turn or exit, or came close to missing it, because you weren't paying enough attention to the here and now? How many fender benders and other more serious traffic accidents occur because drivers are mentally somewhere else rather than focused on the present moment? Not being present-centered interferes with attention and performance to the point where it can become a form of impairment.

Our minds are like an untrained puppy, running all over, not listening, rapidly stopping and starting, changing direction repeatedly, chewing on things, making messes, startling easily and even more easily getting distracted (squirrel!), searching for the next interesting/attractive/pleasurable object, and leaving puddles and piles where it's not supposed to.

The human mind continuously produces thoughts and images, the majority of which have nothing to do with our present-moment circumstances. These thoughts and images grab our attention and run with it, dragging us from one thought to the next, often in rapid-fire succession. This unremitting mental activity regularly takes the form of stories our heads tell us, seductively drawing our attention away from what we intend to focus on and what we are doing.

Many of these stories are compelling tales that pull us back into the past—to events from earlier today, yesterday, last week, last month, last year, or many years ago; or they propel us forward into the future to things that might or (in all likelihood) might not happen—later today, tomorrow, in two weeks, in six months, or years from now. They invariably distract and detract from our ability to pay conscious attention and respond skillfully to our current circumstances, whether we're holding a conversation, driving, interacting with our kids, or writing a book.

This phenomenon occurs with such stunning regularity that for many, if not most, people, it's standard operating procedure. Most of the time, we don't even realize we're engaged in it. It happens automatically and unconsciously. We are somewhere other than here and now, and it disconnects us from life in the present. When this disconnect happens, wherever we are physically, we are somewhere else mentally and emotionally. And, whomever we're with, we may be mentally and emotionally with other people altogether. When we aren't paying conscious attention to the present moment, we are effectively sleepwalking, even when we're wide-awake. When we're focused on the past or the future, we are cut off from the possibilities inherent in this moment—unable to see and experience it for what it is, separated from the opportunities it presents. Whenever we're unconsciously in the grip of the there and then, it's impossible to be skillful in the here and now.

Mindfulness Is Mind Training

Mindfulness practice trains the mind to come when you call it, to sit and stay. After a time (often an impressively short time) it will naturally wander off, and when it does, you can notice, call it to come back, and it will. Through mindfulness practices, you can develop greater present-moment awareness, along with the ability to direct—and keep—your attention where you want it. The more you anchor your attention in the present, tuned in to the realities of your current situation, the more opportunities you have to make wise choices and engage in intentional and skillful responses.

There are many ways in which staying in the present—in this moment, right here and right now—promotes health and healing. It frees you from the prisons of the past and fantasies of the future. It bestows respite from being trapped in the emotions associated with past events, such as resentment, guilt, shame, and regret, as well as those linked with the future, primarily anxiety and fear.

Everyone has a past, and it's okay and even healthy to visit it from time to time in order to better understand it, put it in perspective, and learn from it. And obviously, looking at and planning for the future is important and positive. But when you spend so much time in the past or the future that your conscious focus is consistently diverted from the here and now, it becomes problematic. Besides, until someone learns how to change the past, it's as good as it's ever going to get. It's impossible to change what happened yesterday or know with any certainty what will happen tomorrow.

Fortunately, the potential for learning, growing, and healing exists in each and every moment. Even though you may have spent the last few minutes somewhere else—in the past or the future—as soon as you become aware of it, you can make a conscious choice to shift your attention to the present.

Recovery, and indeed life, occurs one day at a time. But actually, they happen one moment at a time. Life is unfurling in this exact moment, right here and right now. Present-centered awareness makes us physically, mentally, emotionally, and spiritually available to utilize the possibilities inherent in this moment and the opportunities for learning and growth it presents. Mindfulness and the related practice of meditation are among the most effective pathways to stay in the moment.

If mindfulness is unfamiliar to you, the following simple exercise will give you a practical sense of the experience of it. If you're conversant with mindfulness, as you know, there's no such thing as too much practice. By practicing this exercise and the others located throughout this and the following chapter, you will begin to develop (or deepen) the skill of training your mind to be here now and focus your attention on what you intend.

Focus your attention on your breath. Consciously observe the natural flow of your breathing. Follow your breath as it comes in on your inhale and goes out on your exhale. If your mind starts to wander, gently bring it back to the sensation of your breathing and what you see, hear, or feel.

1. Look around and notice three things you can see; closely observe their size, shape, color, and texture.

2. Listen carefully and notice three things you can hear. While your initial reaction may be that there aren't three different sounds within your range of hearing, if you focus your attention (closing your eyes may help) and quiet your mind, you'll be able to find them. Tune in to the quality and volume of these sounds

3. Notice three things you can feel in contact with your body (your feet on the ground, your clothing on certain parts of your body, the sun on your face, the air against your skin, your back against the chair, etc.). Connect to the nuances of these tactile sensations.

In and around twelve-step meetings, people describe the process of recovery as simple but far from easy. Mindfulness is also fundamentally simple in concept and practice; however, it is light-years away from easy to accomplish. Remaining present-centered is an ongoing challenge. Even people with years of practice (myself included) frequently stray unintentionally, however briefly, into the past or the future.

In fact, because the ongoing parade of thoughts our minds produce is so hypnotic, it's almost impossible to "stay" in this moment constantly. Consequently, training the mind must involve consciously recognizing when you drift away from the here and now and using that awareness to return to it. The work lies not so much in staying in the present moment as in returning to it—over and over and over again. This is another way in which the journey *is* the destination.

Mindfulness and Recovery

While the practice of mindfulness can be beneficial for everyone, it can be especially valuable for people in recovery. By facilitating conscious awareness with a nonjudgmental perspective, mindfulness decreases the vicious circles of anxiety, fear, anger, sadness, depression, guilt, regret, and shame that make so many recovering people so vulnerable to relapse.

Because cravings/urges to use pose a potential threat to recovery, most people have extremely negative reactions to these thoughts and feelings, and they naturally try to avoid or suppress them. However, attempting to avoid or escape cravings only makes them stronger and last longer. Through mindfulness practices, individuals in recovery can better separate themselves from addictive thoughts and emotional attachments to the object(s) of their addiction by consciously observing their urges to use with an open and curious attitude, from a place of accepting, nonjudgmental awareness.

When an uncomfortable feeling like a craving or anxiety arises, people who practice mindfulness are better able to recognize their discomfort and observe it with presence and compassion, instead of automatically looking for something—alcohol or other drugs, food, sex, shopping, gambling, social media, etc.—in which to submerge it.

The practice of mindfulness stimulates the understanding that thoughts and feelings, including urges to escape, numb, and avoid by using, are always temporary. Through mindfulness and meditation, it is possible to learn how to face uncomfortable, painful thoughts, feelings, and physical sensations—learning to accept the pain, anxiety, anger, or sadness and let it pass—without obsessing or needing to change them, including by using.

Emotional Contagion Is Bilateral

The energy and emotional states of people with whom we are in close physical and emotional proximity invariably affect us. These states can be unconsciously seductive and contagious. For example, when you're with someone you care about and he or she is upset or agitated, you may begin to become upset and agitated. Conversely, if you're with someone who's calm, you're likely to become calmer.

This is especially true with children and their parents. Research indicates that the stress parents feel typically elevates the stress levels of the children in their care, in ways that can undermine those children's psychological and intellectual development. Young children in particular are greatly influenced by the emotional states of their parents, not only due to their physical dependence upon them but also because their age-appropriate narcissism results in thinking their parents' distress is about them. The good news is that when parents learn the skills needed to create consistent, nurturing home environments, their children's stress levels frequently decrease while emotional intelligence and psychological resilience improve.[11]

When parents can tolerate and simply be present with their own intense emotions, along with the intense emotions of their children, the children learn that their emotions aren't so scary and don't have to overwhelm them. Children can then begin to better tolerate their own feelings—a critical emotional regulation skill.

Mindfulness as an Operating System Upgrade

As described in Chapter Three, childhood attachment experiences have profound impacts on our mental-emotional architecture and our capacity for healthy relationships. Many of the beneficial effects of mindfulness and meditation bear a remarkable resemblance to the characteristics of people who grow up with healthy, attuned attachments. In this way, mindfulness practice can effectively upgrade our internal operating system.

A computer's operating system (OS) enables the hardware to operate and communicate with the software. Hardware includes the physical components of a computer system—the central processing unit (CPU), keyboard, hard drive, power supply, etc. Software

---

11 Paul Tough, "To Help Kids Thrive, Coach Their Parents," *New York Times* (May 21, 2016). http://www. nytimes.com/2016/05/22/opinion/sunday/to-help-kids-thrive-coach-their-parents.html?emc=edit_ th_20160522&nl=todaysheadlines&nlid=53091940.

refers to organized collections of computer data and instructions and consists of programs that permit a computer to perform specific tasks, such as online searches, email, word processing, and anti-virus protection. The operating system is the core set of programs that runs the computer and upon which all other programs rely on in order to operate.

Human hardware includes the brain, nervous system, and the body, while the software consists of our thoughts, emotions, and physical sensations. The human OS consists of our relationship to others, ourselves, and the world around us as well as our spiritual connection. It assigns meaning to our thoughts, emotions, and physical sensations; mediates between our internal and external experiences; links our neurophysiology with our thoughts and feelings; and determines the quality of our interactions. Operating system updates correct program incompatibilities, discovered errors, and security vulnerabilities. Operating system upgrades improve overall functioning.

Mindfulness can upgrade your internal operating system by helping to make the unconscious conscious and create the space for reasoned and skillful responses, even in the face of highly charged feelings. Stress, anxiety, fear, and anger lose their grip more easily and quickly, giving you greater freedom of choice to respond intentionally rather than to react reflexively. Mindfulness promotes emotional regulation and mitigates impulsivity by increasing the gap between stimulus (what happens to us) and response (what we do with what happens to us). The crucial importance of this gap is vividly encapsulated in a paraphrase of Viktor Frankl's description in *Man's Search for Meaning* of how he survived the horrors of life in a Nazi death camp during World War II: between stimulus and response there is a space. In that space is the opportunity to choose our response. In our response lies our growth and our freedom.

Mindfulness Improves Emotional Intelligence

Increasing emotional intelligence is part of how mindfulness practice upgrades your internal operating system. Unlike IQ or formal intelligence/intellect, which is generally fixed and stable throughout life, emotional intelligence (EI) refers to a range of internal and interpersonal skills that can be acquired and improved with practice. Although some people are naturally more emotionally intelligent than others, you can develop high emotional intelligence even if you weren't born with it.

Internal EI skills include the ability to identify one's own emotions, be consciously aware of them as they happen, and regulate them and their effects on one's behavior. Interpersonal or interactional EI skills include the ability to accurately sense and empathize with the emotions of other people and use the awareness of your own emotions and those of others to negotiate interactions skillfully. These skills are part and parcel of mindfulness practice.

Emotional intelligence requires effective communication between the rational-logical part of the brain—the prefrontal cortex—and the emotional part of the brain centered in the amygdala within the limbic system. Mindfulness is a bridge that connects these two areas of the brain, and consistent practice of these skills builds new neural pathways that over time become stronger and more efficient.

Mindfulness can help you better tolerate and stay with difficult emotions, so they don't hold you hostage. You can increase your ability to bear discomfort—physically and emotionally—and be present with it, without being suffocated by it or needing to push it away. When you enlarge your capacity to bear emotional discomfort, you are less likely to react automatically to your emotions or let them control you.

More people struggle with anxiety than perhaps any other emotion. The word *worry* originates from an old English word for strangle. The anxiety that comes with worrying, with its anticipatory fear of what might or could possibly happen in the future, strangles your ability to be skillful in the here and now.

Mindfulness practice can prepare you to recognize and observe the experience of anxiety, fear, sadness, guilt, depression, loneliness, emptiness, frustration, anger, and other distressing emotions—along with the negative thinking that both contributes to these emotions and is reinforced by them—with acceptance and perspective. As the Buddha observed in the Sutta-Nipāta:

> *If one going down into a river,*
> *swollen and swiftly flowing,*
> *is carried away by the current—*
> *how can one help others across?*

Changing the Structure of Your Experience

All experience has structure. The structure of your experience includes your thoughts and your relationships to those thoughts, your current emotions and your relationship to them, your spiritual connection with that beyond yourself, your physical sensations and your relationship to them, and where you are and who (if anyone) you're with physically. Change any aspect of that structure, and the experience itself will change. This dynamic is evidenced in the observation that when we change the way we look at things, the things we look at change. By helping you learn to relate differently to discomfort—whether that discomfort is physical, mental, or emotional—mindfulness practice can shift the structure of your experience.

Our thoughts occur so naturally and automatically that we see them not as a part of ourselves but *as* ourselves. We can become so closely identified with our thoughts that we are completely unaware of any separation: our thoughts are us, and we are our thoughts. We also tend to believe in the inherent accuracy of our thoughts: *I think it; therefore it is true.* Assuming our thoughts are facts, that they are true and valid without examination, frequently leads to bio-psycho-spiritual imbalance and contributes to suffering.

So-called "normal" people unafflicted with addiction or other challenging chronic conditions can ruminate on something by continuously and unproductively replaying it in their minds or magnifying the negative aspects of it, exaggerating its significance. In this unconscious autopilot mode, we mentally manufacture impressive stories about what might or could happen. These narratives are usually worse (sometimes much worse) than what actually happens. As William Shakespeare wrote in *Hamlet*, "There is nothing either good or bad, but thinking makes it so."

The more consciously aware of these unhelpful thought processes you become, the more you can develop the capacity to observe, question, dispute, accept, or (if you choose to) adjust your thinking. When you cultivate the practice of paying close attention to your thoughts and the way you talk to yourself, you tend to misguide yourself less often.

Cognitive defusion is a mindfulness-based practice within Acceptance and Commitment Therapy (ACT) that focuses on observing and accepting distressing thoughts without buying into or attaching any particular value to them. By facilitating detached witnessing, cognitive defusion changes the nature of the relationship you have with your thoughts and thought process.

Mindfulness is a state of direct contact—unobstructed by thoughts, emotions, and physical sensations—with yourself and the world around you. Ironically, allowing yourself to observe, feel, accept, express, and coexist with uncomfortable, often painful, emotions takes less energy than running from or stifling them, which makes more energy available for attuned parenting-supportive pursuits. Emotional balance occurs when you can feel whatever comes up, without suppressing or being overwhelmed by it, and learn to accept those feelings without judgment.

Parenting evokes emotions that swing from the beautiful to the brutal, sometimes at high speed. Most parents spend considerable time in the realm of the bittersweet. It's a phenomenal challenge to keep our heart open to the suffering of others, especially to that of our children, while maintaining a quiet and self-aware mind. Through the practice of mindfulness, you can acquire the capacity to rise to that challenge. Only through conscious awareness can you step back from the in-your-face immediacy of your experience to bear calmer witness to and be present with all its joys and sorrows.

N. O. A. H. S.

I developed N.O.A.H.S. as a mindfulness practice to handle uncomfortable, distressing emotions more skillfully. It follows the following sequence: **Notice** & **Name** the feeling(s) > **Observe** it > **Allow** it > **Hold** it > put **Space** around it. This practice can be used with any difficult or painful emotional state and involves several levels of awareness and action.

The first is to *notice*, to become consciously aware, that you are experiencing an uncomfortable emotion. Although initially you may not know specifically what the emotion is, it is important to definitively notice and acknowledge that you are experiencing an emotion.

The next step is to identify the particular emotion, to *name* it. A fundamental part of discerning specific emotions from a mass of intense or vague feelings is to put them into words and give them a name. Say to yourself, *I feel anxious*, or *I feel angry*, or *I feel sad, depressed, guilty, lonely, afraid, etc.* Sometimes we feel more than one emotion at a time: *I feel frustrated and disappointed.*

If you struggle to identify and name your emotions, start by making the connection between different emotions and where you feel them in your body. Learning how you register different emotions in your body in terms of their location (where you feel them) and sensation (what they feel like) will enable you to identify them more quickly and accurately. For example, anger may be felt as tightness in your shoulders, sadness as an aching in your chest, fear as a knot in your stomach, and joy as warmth in your heart.

Observe the emotion. Gently rest your awareness on it and view it with openhearted interest.

Allow the emotion (whatever it may be) to simply be. Let yourself feel it without needing to fight against it, run from it, or cling to it.

Hold the emotion. Breathe into it, be present with it, coexist with it, and make peace with it.

Put *space* around it. Visualize putting space in the form of distance or some sort of perimeter or border around it.

And notice what happens.

This practice encompasses elements of emotional regulation, distress tolerance, self-compassion, and self-acceptance. In facilitating a more detached witness perspective with our uncomfortable emotions, we can be present with them and yet gain some separation from them, providing the space to experience them differently. It changes our relationship to them, and as described previously, in changing the structure of the experience, the experience itself changes. As a result, whenever I use this practice, the emotions with which I'm challenged almost always become a little smaller and begin to dissipate.

The entire progression of this practice can take as long as you require, but it need not take more than about a minute or two. At this point in my practice, I usually go through it in about thirty seconds.

Whether pleasurable, painful, or neutral, your emotions are an intrinsic part of who you are. You can't disavow your distressing emotions without disavowing part of yourself. Self-acceptance depends on finding ways to accept and make peace with those parts of yourself that you dislike and with which you are uncomfortable. If you want to be able to help your children acquire the gift of self-acceptance, you need to have it yourself. You can't teach what you don't know, and you can't give what you don't have.

6

MEDITATION AND OTHER SPECIFIC MINDFULNESS PRACTICES

The real voyage of discovery consists not in seeking new landscapes, but in having new eyes.

Marcel Proust

What's the Difference between Meditation and Mindfulness?

In some contexts, the terms *mindfulness* and *meditation* seem to be used interchangeably. Both meditation and mindfulness have roots in ancient traditions and share the common goal of facilitating the experience of being more present-centered, calmer, more focused, less reactive, and less stressed. They complement each other and overlap in many ways. Mindfulness and meditation both provide practitioners a vast array of mental, emotional, physical, and spiritual benefits.

In understanding the relationship between them, it may be helpful to think of meditation as a subset of mindfulness. Meditation is a set of techniques for practicing mindfulness using a particular structure. Forms of it are found in many spiritual and some religious traditions. Meditation utilizes various practices that quiet the mind, usually through sitting still for dedicated amounts of time (a few minutes to a half hour or more). However, meditation goes beyond sitting practice. Mindfulness, on the other hand, can be practiced within or outside of formal meditation and woven into any activity. Eating a meal, washing the dishes, vacuuming the floor, taking a walk, and being in conversation with your children are all opportunities to practice mindfulness.

Intentional Breathing

Breathing is the most direct way to bring the mind together with the body. A Chinese proverb suggests, "If you know the art of breathing you have the strength, wisdom, and courage of ten tigers." As the lynchpin in the mind-body connection, breathing anchors all mindfulness practices as well as most forms of meditation. It happens automatically—you don't have to think about breathing to stay alive; it just happens. However, it is also one of the very few involuntary bodily functions over which you can exert intentional influence; you can deliberately modify how you breathe in ways that promote health, well-being, and mindful awareness. Breathing intentionally is one of the most elemental yet powerful ways to bring yourself to present-moment awareness, quiet the mind, and self-calm.

When you breathe in deeply on your inhale, you take more air into your lungs, which means more oxygen enters the bloodstream, where it circulates throughout the body to the brain and vital organs. Breathing out fully upon exhale expels more carbon dioxide (CO_2)—a waste product generated as your body uses up oxygen—from your body. When CO_2 accumulates in the body past a certain point, it causes adverse effects on nervous system, respiratory, and cardiac functioning. So when you don't exhale completely, carbon dioxide remains in the body and accumulates in your cells, producing fatigue and causing you to yawn, diminishing mental clarity and increasing stress. Exhaling fully also makes it easier to breathe in more oxygen on the subsequent inhale.

The combination of consciously breathing in deeply and breathing out fully deactivates the sympathetic division of the autonomic nervous system and turns off the body's stress response while simultaneously engaging the parasympathetic division and triggering the relaxation response. As a result, muscle tension, heart rate, and blood pressure decrease; digestion improves; immune system function increases, and the whole body moves toward a greater state of relaxation. When oxygenated blood flow to the brain increases, it creates a calming effect, along with an increase in energy and concentration.

When we feel anxious, fearful, stressed, or otherwise in pain, our breathing becomes rapid and shallow; therefore, people who consistently feel anxious and stressed may actually be chronically under-breathing, taking mostly quick, shallow breaths. In contrast, when our breathing becomes slower and deeper, we experience decreases in anxiety, fear, stress, and pain. In this way, intentional breathing can help regulate the central nervous system.

Learn and practice breathing intentionally. Teach it to your children and practice with them. It is one of the most valuable skills you can build for yourself and share with your children.

Intentional breathing practice

- Consciously tune in to and observe your breathing.

- Become more aware of breathing in on your inhale and out on your exhale.

- As you breathe, place the front of your tongue on the roof of your mouth slightly behind your top front teeth. According to the Chinese health paradigm—which includes practices as diverse as acupuncture, Tai Chi, and Chi Kung—having your tongue on the roof of your mouth continuously stimulates and balances the body's primary energy meridians. It also allows saliva to flow more naturally, decreasing the need to swallow.

- If at all possible, breathe through your nose. Breathing through the nose tends to be smoother, and quieter. If for any reason you can't breathe through your nose, it's perfectly okay to breathe through your mouth.

- Allow your breathing to become slower, deeper, and quieter.

- Exhale completely, squeezing out as much air as you can before beginning your next inhale.

- Breathe abdominally—breathing in through the stomach rather than the chest brings more oxygen into the body. Some people find it helpful to put their hand on their stomach as an anchor. So when they inhale, their stomach pushes their hand outward, and their exhale brings their hand in toward their spine.

- If you notice your attention drifting, gently bring your awareness back to your breath, continuing to breathe slowly and deeply.

4-7-8 breathing

This specific technique can be helpful for anyone who needs more structure in his or her intentional breathing practice.

- Inhale through your nose for a count of four seconds. When you inhale for four seconds, you force yourself to take in more oxygen.

- Hold your breath for seven seconds. Briefly holding your breath allows the oxygen to spread throughout your bloodstream and has the added benefit of a slight boost in alertness and energy.

- Exhale through your mouth for a count of eight seconds. This allows you to expel more carbon dioxide from your lungs steadily and completely.

Meditation

Meditation is the most well-known method of achieving a state of mindfulness, the rock star of mindfulness practices. Meditation is a skill that helps quiet the mind by turning down the volume and quantity of the ongoing thought-based chatter in our head, giving us greater opportunity to tune in to the present moment. Although it can be beneficial for everyone, practicing meditation is highly recommended for people in recovery, so much so that it is a central part of the Eleventh Step in twelve-step programs.

Meditation connects the mind with the body and precipitates greater feelings of calm, stimulating the body's relaxation response by activating the parasympathetic division of the autonomic nervous system. The parasympathetic division handles rest, relaxation, recharge, and conservation of energy. Upon its activation, breathing slows and deepens, muscles soften, metabolism and pulse rate slow, and blood pressure decreases.

One of the main reasons that meditation has been around for over 2,500 years is that, in essence, it's extremely simple. Ironically, because life is so complicated for so many people, the simplicity of meditation can actually make it more challenging. The purpose of meditation is to set aside the distractions that continuously clamor for your attention and consciously slow down your mind—starting with your thoughts—to bring you to this moment, here and now.

There are many ways to meditate, and it's important to find an approach that fits for you. Most forms of meditation fall within the following three fundamental structures, one of which is based directly on mindfulness.

- **Mindfulness meditation:** centers conscious attention on the big picture of internal and external sensations using a relaxed, though focused, observation of thoughts, emotions, and bodily sensations as they arise and fall.

- **Breathing meditation:** concentrates on the breath and makes it the locus of attention using intentional breathing as described earlier.

- **Mantra meditation:** anchors conscious attention on a mantra, an energy-based sound that produces a specific physical vibration, and may or may not have a specific meaning. The word *mantra* means to free yourself from your mind. It originates from two Sanskrit words: *manas*, or mind, and *trai*, meaning to free from or liberate.

Other types of meditation focus on bringing to awareness and expanding the felt experience of specific beneficial spiritual principles and emotional states such as compassion, loving-kindness, equanimity, gratitude, or patience. You bring these emotional states to mind and either turn them inward toward yourself or outward in general or toward specific others. Guided meditations, in which you follow recorded voice suggestions to help you access meditative states, are available in digital formats on a variety of web-based platforms.

Several guidelines apply to all forms of meditation.

- **Find a quiet space:** Meditation is most effective (more so for beginners) when there are minimal environmental distractions. And since focused attention is an essential ingredient, as much as you can, try to find a tranquil space for the duration of your meditation.

- **Assume a comfortable position:** Because muscle tension can disrupt attention and interfere with the relaxation response, physical comfort is important. You can use any position, but sitting in a chair or on a firm pillow or rug with your head, neck, and back straight is recommended. Lying down to meditate is generally not suggested as many people have a tendency to become too drowsy and fall asleep.

- **Be aware that when you first start to meditate, it may seem strange and awkward:** This may be the case, especially if it is difficult for you to be still both mentally and physically. It's often best to begin slowly, perhaps with three to five minutes a day, and gradually work up to fifteen to twenty minutes.

- **When breathing, close your mouth, place your tongue loosely on the roof of your mouth, and breathe smoothly through your nose:** Follow the guidelines detailed in the section on Intentional Breathing—breathing deeply and slowly through your stomach rather than your chest and exhaling completely in preparation for the next inhale.

- **Consistency is key:** If at all possible, try to meditate every day, at the same time of day, in the same location. In this way, you develop a pattern and rhythm for your meditation practice that will help establish it as a habit. Morning works well for many people because it sets a tone for the day; for others evening works better because it helps them wind down. Most importantly, meditate regularly, even when you don't feel like it or think you don't have time for it. A few minutes may not seem like much, but it's infinitely better than nothing.

A common question beginners ask is, "How do I stop my thoughts?" The simple answer is that you don't. Self-imposed pressure to stop thoughts mobilizes both resistance and judgment, which work against meditation's fundamental intent. Even during meditation, other thoughts—including those related to the past or future—naturally intrude. This is neither positive nor negative; it simply is.

When your mind wanders (and it will), the most helpful thing you can do is to become aware of the thoughts and simply notice and observe them, without judging either the thoughts or yourself for having them. You can watch them pass like birds flying overhead.

There is no need to be disturbed by them, obsess over them, or try to change them; simply become aware that you have drifted away from the moment and matter-of-factly refocus your attention and return to the here-and-now.

Similarly, if there are external noises or sounds related to other people or the environment, you can pay as much or as little attention to them as you like. You can take note of them, accept them and any thoughts or feelings you have related to them, and bring your attention back to the focus of your meditation, returning your awareness to the present moment.

Meditation and mindfulness practice become even more important in a culture that is increasingly Attention Deficit Disorder-inducing. Seductive technology-driven distractions encourage and normalize spreading ourselves ever thinner. The proliferation of twenty-four-seven connectivity, expanding mobile information technology, and new social media platforms places ever-greater demands on our precious attention, emotional availability, time, and energy. How common has it become for people to be plugged in to their smartphones, tablets, and other devices, absorbed in electronic pacification, completely disassociated from where they are and who they are with?

There are myriad health benefits associated with the practices of mindfulness and meditation that have been demonstrated by scientific research over the last three decades. Although these positive effects begin almost immediately, they also accumulate over time.

Interestingly, however, while science has documented the wide-ranging and specific positive impacts that mindfulness and meditation have on health and wellness, relatively little has been known about the specific neurobiological effects of cultivating present-moment awareness that underlie these benefits—until recently.

A 2016 study by researchers from Carnegie Mellon University found that internal inflammation seems to be the central factor. Mindfulness practice reduces inflammation by causing particular changes in the brain's functional connectivity. Chronic inflammation—the persistent, ongoing activation of the immune system's defense response, even in the absence of injury or infection—is at the heart of many serious health problems, including cancer, heart disease, diabetes, stroke, depression, and Alzheimer's disease.[12]

The numerous physical and mental health benefits of mindfulness and meditation, along with the empirical research that substantiates them, are detailed in the Appendix at the end of this book.

Mini-Mindfulness Practices

Mindfulness practice doesn't necessitate special settings or large blocks of time. There are many ways to incorporate it in the ordinary tasks and activities of everyday life. You can create many different opportunities to consciously anchor your awareness in the here and now and access a few moments of mindfulness throughout the course of your day. Once again, small pebbles can make big ripples.

1. Although multitasking may be unavoidable at times, the daily experience of pressure to "get things done" unconsciously ensnares many people in its gravitational pull. Multitasking frequently becomes standard operating procedure, even when it isn't necessary. Strive to minimize multitasking and do one thing at a time; be present with the task at hand, giving it your undiluted attention.

2. Do it deliberately and without hurrying—even if you're in a rush. As John Wooden, the legendary UCLA basketball coach, regularly instructed his players, "Be quick, but don't hurry."

3. Do it to completion.

4. Give yourself permission to do less than what you may have planned or what your thinking says you "should do" or "have to do."

---

12 J. David Creswell, et al., "Alterations in Resting-State Functional Connectivity Link Mindfulness Meditation with Reduced Interleukin-6: A Randomized Controlled Trial," *Biological Psychiatry*, 80, no. 1 (July 2016): 53–61.

5. Put space—even a brief pause—between the things you do rather than going directly from one activity to the next.

6. Each time you scroll through Facebook, Twitter, Instagram, or other social media platforms, pause on a random name (be it someone you know or not) and take a moment to wish that person well—perhaps literally saying to yourself: _____, *may you be well. May you be at peace.*

7. As you wake up from sleep, take a moment while lying in bed with your eyes open and express appreciation for the gift of waking up to another day. Not everyone receives this gift.

8. When you first step outside in the morning, take a few seconds to observe—without judgment—the sights and sounds of your neighborhood.

9. When you approach a window in your home or office, take a few moments to pause, look through it, and really notice what you see.

Mindful Eating

Many people, both in and out of recovery, eat emotionally—that is, they eat in response to stress or emotional discomfort (anxiety, fear, loneliness, boredom, anger, or sadness). Sometimes, this is also an attempt to fill a sense of internal emptiness. When people behave this way, they eat without thinking about what or why they're eating; they may not even taste the food, which they chew quickly and incompletely. Have you ever finished eating something only to realize you don't know how it tasted?

Mindful eating is the antithesis of stressed or emotional eating and the antidote for it. Mindful eating means paying conscious attention to the experience of eating using all the senses. It emphasizes the awareness of taste, as well as colors, textures, smells, and sounds, during the process of eating. For instance, when mindfully eating an apple, you might notice the color, feel how smooth it is, take in its fragrance, listen to what it sounds like when you bite into it, and taste it fully, one bite at a time.

By making the experience of taking food and drink into the body much more conscious, eating mindfully slows the process of ingesting, tasting, chewing, and swallowing. The intent is to pay close and careful attention to the sensory aspects of your food and the process of eating and to eat deliberately rather than unconsciously shoveling food into your face. The result is that you will eat more slowly, taste your food more thoroughly, chew your food more completely, and swallow it more patiently. All of this contributes to healthier digestion. Over time, this practice— even if you only engage in it occasionally—can help you change your relationship with food to one that is more present-centered, satisfying, and healthier.

- Before you eat, bring your awareness to the activity. Are you actually hungry and need nourishment in preparation for some activity, or are you eating out of some sort of emotional dis-ease?

- As much as possible, try to eat before you get to the point of being extremely hungry.

- Take two or three deep breaths to relax and connect your mind with your body.

- Appreciate the food you're getting ready to eat.

- Consider what it took to get that food from its origins to your table.

- As you eat, notice the aroma(s), texture(s), and color(s) of your food.

- Take one bite at a time, tasting it fully.

- Chew your food carefully, savoring it.

- Swallow it slowly.

- Wait until you've completely swallowed one bite of your food before taking the next one.

- Pause briefly and take an intentional breath—in and out—between swallowing and taking that next bite.

- As you eat, remind yourself to breathe.

- Pay attention to when you feel satisfied or *begin* to feel "full."

- Stop eating when you reach this point, rather than continuing to eat until you feel "stuffed" and uncomfortable.

- If there is food left, store it for another time.

- Notice how you feel when you are finished eating.

Practice the skill of mindful eating, teach it to your children, and practice it with them.

Mindful Walking

When you walk, how much do you consciously consider the process of walking? In general, how much actual attention do you pay to where you are and the physical aspects of the process? To what extent do you really watch where you're going? A remarkable number of people today pay little conscious attention to how and where they walk. How many people do you see focusing more on their phones than on where they place their feet?

Mindful walking is a form of walking meditation, a process of bringing present-moment attention to the act of walking, wherever you may be. You walk while anchoring your conscious awareness in each step and can practice this anywhere: in your home, at work, while shopping, in a crowded urban area, or out in nature. As Thich Nhat Hanh, the venerable Vietnamese Buddhist monk once nominated for the Nobel Peace Prize by Martin Luther King, Jr., encourages, "Walk as if you are kissing the Earth with your feet."

Initially, it's best to learn this practice by walking back and forth between two points about fifteen to twenty feet apart. The beginning practice will help you get a feel for the experience of walking mindfully.

- While standing still, become aware of your body and how it feels. Feel your feet on the ground.

- Allow your knees to bend slightly.

- Take two to three deep breaths and bring your awareness into the present moment.

- Begin to walk slowly, so you can tune in to the particulars of the process of walking.

- Walk at a pace that allows you to feel the direct sensations of your legs and feet moving.

- With each step, bring your awareness to the act of lifting your foot, followed by stepping your foot on the ground.

- To keep your attention connected with the sensations of walking, you may find it helpful to repeat the following phrase to yourself: *Lifting, stepping—lifting, stepping—lifting, stepping.*

- Breathe intentionally as you walk.

- Feel the changing sensations in your feet and legs—the shifting of weight, pressure, and movement.

- Although the sensations may feel a bit strange and your walking may seem stiff, try to walk naturally and easily.

- With practice and a more "normal" pace, you may find it helpful to internally say just one word per stride, e.g. *right* then *left, right, left, right, left.*

- When you notice your mind engaged in thoughts or stories, gently bring your awareness back to the sensations of lifting and stepping.

- When you reach the end of your walking path, stop and stand still, taking a few moments to feel your body standing in a neutral state of rest before turning around and beginning to walk in the other direction.

Once you're familiar with the process of mindful walking, you can take this practice anywhere you walk, from the inner city to the mountain wilderness. Practice mindful walking, teach it to your children, and practice it with them.

Urge Surfing for Recovery Maintenance

Urge surfing is a mindfulness practice developed by G. Alan Marlatt, PhD, as part of Mindfulness-Based Relapse Prevention. Urges, cravings, or impulses to engage in the use of substances or activities, similar to waves at the ocean's edge, follow a natural progression— they rise in intensity, reach a crest, crash, and recede.

The conscious awareness mindfulness brings about helps people observe urges or cravings to use alcohol and other drugs (or food, sex, gambling, shopping, etc.), as well as be present with them, accept them, and ride them out rather than fight against the urges or act on them reflexively and unconsciously.

Urge surfing allows cravings to run their course, allowing them to crest and subside by observing without judging them or oneself and accepting them without becoming attached to or trying to suppress them. Left to their own devices, urges or cravings rarely last longer than fifteen to twenty minutes, at which point they pass.

Surf that urge

1. In the same way that skilled surfers scan the ocean looking to pick up waves as soon as they begin to form, you can practice becoming aware of urges early in their genesis. When an urge occurs, notice it consciously. Name it as an urge to use.

2. Observe the internal experiences—the thoughts, emotions, and physical sensations—that comprise the urge. Visualize the urge as a wave. Tune in to your breathing, focusing on making your breathing slower and deeper—breathing in fully and deeply through your abdomen on your inhale and breathing out completely to empty your lungs on your exhale. You can use this form of intentional breathing like a surfboard: be present with the wave as it rises, peaks, and subsides, effectively riding it out.

When the next urge arises, repeat steps one and two. The more you practice this process, the more quickly you'll be able to recognize urges, and the more skilled you'll become at riding them out. Thoughts and feelings, including urges to use substances or activities, are always temporary. The mindfulness practice of urge surfing can help anyone in addiction recovery learn how to bear urges or cravings more skillfully.

The Paradox of Suffering

Suffering is a function of the beliefs people attach to their emotional and physical pain. For instance, whenever someone believes he or she shouldn't be in pain and that pain should be avoided at all costs, the person will experience suffering. Ironically, the harder someone works to avoid the experience of pain, the greater the suffering tends to be.

In *The Wisdom of Insecurity: A Message for an Age of Anxiety,* author and Zen philosopher Alan Watts called this paradox "the backwards law," describing how whenever we actively pursue a specific outcome, it tends to elude us. In other words, the harder we pursue feeling "good," the more attached we are to that outcome, the more emotional pain and suffering we will experience, making it much less likely we'll actually feel good. The intense desire for a more positive experience creates suffering. Mindful awareness of this dynamic, combined with acceptance of our current predicament (with its attendant emotional distress), however, will result in feeling better.

Strategies (including the use of alcohol and other drugs) to feel better through avoidance of distressing experiences and emotions may work temporarily, but inevitably they only boomerang, prolonging and intensifying the discomfort. With its emphasis on acceptance and acknowledgment of the transitory nature of our experiences, mindfulness practice provides a pathway to walk through our challenging experiences—be they internal, external, or interactional. Our distress, like clouds passing overheard, is sometimes thin, light, and sparse and other times thick, dark, and intimidating. But, we need to differentiate between the clouds and the sky.

Mindfulness and Self-Compassion

It's easy to fall prey to the weight of guilt and regret related to specific parenting experiences: things I deeply wish I had or hadn't done, or had done very differently. I dare suggest that this is universal when it comes to parenting, and it is where the mindfulness practices of self-compassion and self-forgiveness can play a critical role.

Self-compassion involves identifying and opening to your own suffering rather than trying to avoid it and exercising self-kindness in response to your inadequacies and failures instead of engaging in harsh judgments and self-criticism. It offers nonjudgmental understanding of your pain, so you appreciate your personal experience as part of the larger human experience.[13] As you may have noticed, mindfulness is inherent in self-compassion.

A simple self-compassion practice that you can do any time you find yourself struggling emotionally is known as the "Self-Compassion Break."[14] It has three stages:

---

13   Kristen Neff, "Self-Compassion: An Alternative Conceptualization of a Healthy Attitude toward Oneself," *Self and Identity,* 2 (2003): 85–101. Psychology Press 1529-8868/2003 DOI: 10.1080/15298860390129863.

14   Greater Good Science Center at the University of California, Berkeley, "Self-Compassion Break," 2015. https://ggia.berkeley.edu/practice/self_compassion_break?utm_source=GGIA+Newsletter+Jan+10+2017&utm_campaign=GGIA+Newsletter+Jan+2017&utm_medium=email#data-tab-how.

- **Be mindful:** With nonjudgmental acceptance, observe your pain and acknowledge it by saying to yourself something along the lines of, *This is a moment of suffering* or *I'm in pain* or *This is distress.*

- **Remember that you're not alone:** All people experience discomfort and distress—it is part of our shared humanity. Reinforce this awareness by saying to yourself, *Suffering is a part of being human;* or *All people experience emotional pain;* or *Everyone struggles at times.*

- **Be kind to yourself:** Consciously express kindness to yourself, internally saying something like, *May I learn to accept myself as I am;* or *May I be at peace, may I be at ease;* or *May I be forgiving toward myself.*

Mindfulness Practice and Values

The connection between our intentions as a reflection of our values and our attention is all too easily weakened or lost, like a cell phone call that loses clarity or gets dropped. While we may start out with strong and clear intentions as parents guided by our values, there are many things that derail or distract us and many reasons we become distanced from them. Mindfulness practice can be instrumental in aligning your attention with your values-based intentions in ways that improve the quality of parent-child interactions.

Too often, we focus on presents instead of presence. Our presence is a precious gift we can give our children at any time, regardless of our financial status. When we give our children our time, attention, and emotional availability, we give them the gift of recognizing their intrinsic value and worthiness.

With the support of mindfulness practice, you can teach your kids the skills of self-awareness, present-moment attention, distress tolerance, and emotional regulation. These skills will equip them to better manage their own inner experiences. The ability to craft even a few moments of internal stillness for themselves allows their nervous systems the opportunity to settle and reset. Neither you nor they have to be ruled by your immediate thoughts and feelings.

Practice Is a Noun as Well as a Verb

I practice mindfulness and meditation, and I have a mindfulness and meditation practice. From day to day, my practice varies in quality, depth, and ease. Some days, I find it easier to actualize conscious present-moment awareness; nonjudgmental witnessing of thoughts, emotions, and physical sensations; and acceptance without attachment or aversion. When this happens, I'm freed from the need to control, guided by and able to flow with the river of life today. I'm gifted with learning how to live more selflessly, with an awakened mind and an open heart, with a heart full of gratitude and a mind free of expectations, seeing all beings (including myself) with eyes of compassion. Other days, these experiences are fleeting and hard to come by.

Mindfulness and meditation practice doesn't require you to show up happy, enthusiastic, or serene. You can show up with a busy, crazed mind and a heavy heart. You just have to show up and be present.

When parents practice mindfulness, it nurtures their children's roots. When they teach mindfulness practices to their children, it strengthens their wings.

7

CONNECTION THROUGH COMMUNICATION: PART I

We have become ready to understand rather than to be understood.

Narcotics Anonymous, Sixth Edition

The process of communication helps us to connect more fully with others. Healthy, effective communication involves conscious awareness and a set of skills that can be learned and practiced. In recovery, the importance of communicating with others is reinforced in many ways. Those of us in twelve-step programs are encouraged and supported to share what's going on in our lives—our challenges and successes, our experience, our strength and hope—in meetings, with our more immediate circles of support, with our sponsors, and with our sponsees (if we sponsor others).

The way in which we learn how to communicate in recovery is unusual in that we support each other in exposing the soft underbelly of our vulnerabilities and practice being present with them. When it works well, twelve-step recovery—much like quality psychotherapy—provides an environment where people feel safe enough to share parts of themselves and the experiences they have previously kept hidden behind a wall of secret-keeping and psychological defenses (denial, minimization, avoidance, rationalization, reaction-formation, and my personal favorite, intellectualization).

Most parents don't have access to such environments. As a person in recovery, you have a frame of reference for how this process works and a foundation that prepares you to create at least some elements of this "therapeutic environment" in your communication with your children, regardless of their age and stage of development.

When it works well, communication generates a connection between people that allows for an exchange of thoughts, ideas, and feelings and leads to new learning and deeper understanding. This exchange is evidenced by a speaker sending a message, which a listener hears, understands, and to which he or she accurately (and ideally, empathically) responds. It seems simple, but it isn't.

People tend to take the communication process for granted. We generally figure that the communication between two or more people is no big deal. It just works. We're inclined to assume that "you're picking up what I'm putting down" and vice versa. However, in reality, the process of communication is impressively complex, even between adults in matter-of-fact circumstances.

Several factors determine whether or not a specific communication experience is likely to be successful in engendering connection and understanding: internal factors that affect each person participating in the communication process individually, interactional factors that affect how two or more people send and receive information, and external factors that affect the extent to which the physical environment is conducive to effective communication.

Communication between adults and children or teens is additionally complicated by the differences in developmental level and brain development and the consequent gaps in the capacity for information processing and understanding. And because communication between parents and their kids is further influenced by the emotional intensity of the parent-child relationship, it requires special care.

The following information, suggestions, and guidance will help you achieve the awareness and build the skills necessary to maximize the potential for you to connect and communicate with your kids in ways that are helpful and healthy. By paying attention with intention to this material, you can decrease the likelihood of misunderstanding and conflict with your kids and facilitate an experience of mutual connection in which they (and you) feel heard, understood, and accepted.

If you work a program of recovery, you know well that feeling heard, understood, and accepted—with all of your imperfections—is a great gift. By paying conscious attention and applying certain skills in your interactions with your kids, you can also give this gift to them.

When you bring mindfulness practices and the spiritual principles of patience, kindness, compassion, and empathy to bear in communicating with your kids, you create the conditions conducive to connection and mutual understanding. It's important to note that mutual understanding doesn't equal agreement, however. Sometimes mutual understanding involves the realization and acceptance that the individuals communicating have fundamentally different positions. Agreeing to disagree is actually a form of achieving mutual understanding.

Communication Principles

There are four fundamental principles intrinsic to the process of communication:

1. The message sent is not necessarily the message received.

2. It is impossible not to communicate.

3. Every message has both content and feeling.

4. Nonverbal cues are more believable than verbal cues.

The message sent is not necessarily the message received

People often assume that just because they say something (or think or intend something) when another person misunderstands (or doesn't understand) or fails to comply with their wishes, it's the other person's fault. After all, the person who sends the message knows exactly what he or she meant. However, what the person on the receiving end of the message hears and understands may be quite different. In contrast to being anyone's "fault," this is among the ways the communication process can go off track.

The message sent may not be the message received because it must pass through the filter of thoughts and feelings—for both sender and receiver. As a result, if you come home from work frustrated, stressed, anxious, irritable, angry, or otherwise upset, you may communicate frustration, anger, or impatience to your children, even though that isn't your intent. The message must also pass through the listener's own filter of thoughts and feelings. To what extent are your kids accustomed to you coming home frustrated, stressed out, sullen, or irritable? If a child expects a parent to be angry or impatient, he or she may hear neutral or even positive statements as harsh or angry.

There is considerable room for misunderstanding between what the speaker intended to say, what he or she actually says, and what the listener hears. The less conscious attention the speaker or the listener pays when sending and receiving the message, and the more emotionally-charged the subject, the more likely there will be a misunderstanding between speaker and listener. Again, communication is further complicated by the differences between adults and kids in developmental level, brain development, and the ability to process information.

The only way to be certain that the message you send is the same one the other person receives is to check this through a process of feedback. This is more critical when dealing with kids, when what you're communicating is of special importance, or you sense (by virtue of verbal or nonverbal reactions) that the other person is unclear or confused.

Checking out the accuracy of your communication involves literally asking what your child heard you say. If what he or she reports hearing does not match up with what you intended, you can then clarify your message by sharing specifically what it was you intended to say. Then you can ask for feedback again, checking out what he or she heard this time around. This process may seem cumbersome, but it results in more clear and accurate communication. Sometimes you may need to go through two or three rounds to ensure that the speaker and listener are on the same page.

It is impossible not to communicate.

All actions—both intentional and unintentional—communicate certain messages. For example, deliberately ignoring someone—particularly your children—is not a case of *not communicating*. Quite the contrary, this action sends a strong message. Moreover, verbal communication (the words one uses) is only one part of the much larger communication process that includes body language, facial expression, tone of voice, and voice volume.

Every message has both content and feeling.

Every message you send consists of content and feeling. The content is what the message is about based on the actual words used. The feeling connected to the content is expressed through nonverbal behavior—body language, gestures, facial expression, tone of voice/inflection, and voice volume.

When discrepancies arise between a message's content and feeling, it naturally creates a degree of confusion for the listener—especially if the content and feeling seem to contradict each other. This confusion is sometimes registered on a conscious level, but it always registers unconsciously. Additionally, it is amplified when the listener is your child, and the younger the child, the more confused and uncertain he or she is likely to be. A classic example of this is when one person says to another, "I'm not mad at you!" (the content) in a terse, loud, and seemingly irritated or angry voice (the feeling).

Nonverbal cues are more believable than verbal cues.

When there's a difference between the content (verbal) and feeling (nonverbal) of a message, the person on the receiving end will almost always give more credibility to the feeling. In other words, if a speaker's words don't match the tone of voice, facial expression, body language, or other nonverbal cues, the listener will pay more attention to and believe the nonverbal behavior.

Consider how you respond when someone gives you what sounds like a compliment, such as "You look great," but with a tone of voice that seems inconsistent with those words or comes across as possibly sarcastic. Are you more likely to believe the verbal (content) or the nonverbal (tone of voice/feeling) cues?

Communication Skills Start with Listening

The importance of listening is obvious when we consider what happens when a partner, parent, or child has something to tell his or her partner, child, or parent and thinks the other person is not listening. Consider how you usually react when you perceive the person to whom you're speaking isn't really listening. What thoughts come to your mind? What feelings come up for you? Think back to what it was like for you when you were a child or teen and you had something to say that you wanted your parent(s) to hear and they weren't listening.

Listening attentively to someone means that you care enough about that person to pay attention to what he or she has to say. It is a powerful form of nonverbal communication that demonstrates respect and value: you view this person as important enough for you to make yourself physically and emotionally available and really focus on what he or she wants to tell you. With your children, making the time and space to really listen to them is one of the most affirming messages you can send—that no matter what it is they have to say, they are worthy of your time and attention. At a less conscious level, this communicates to your children that they have worth as human beings.

Active listening facilitates the experience of being "heard" for the speaker. When you listen to another person with present-centered attention without judging him or her, it also communicates acceptance. This is among the most validating and, in turn, self-acceptance-enhancing experiences a person can have. From the standpoint of promoting self-acceptance and self-esteem in your children, attuned listening (as simple as it may seem) is one of the most beneficial things you can do with and for them.

Obstacles to Listening

A wide range of circumstances—both external and internal—can interfere with people's ability to listen, including

- a lack of interest in what the other person says;

- the listener's own stress or pain (physical or emotional) preoccupies him or her;

- a desire to punish or put the other person down by withholding time and attention;

- being focused on events that occurred in the past or might happen in the future;

- thinking about how to respond when the speaker finishes talking;

- fear that the listener will be expected to change his or her behavior based on what the speaker says;

- attempting to multitask;

- difficulty tolerating and being present with the speaker's expression of strong or distressing emotions.

Many people confuse listening with approval, fearing that listening will be automatically interpreted as agreement, although they are completely separate issues. Listening doesn't commit the listener to anything other than being present and available.

As a gender-based generalization, men (and fathers) tend to be action-oriented and have more difficulty listening to what they interpret as "problems" because they feel they have to fix the situation or do something about it. They tend to underestimate the value of just listening. In most situations, especially with your children, simply taking the time and making the space to listen with care and concern is much more important than "doing" anything.

Listening and Multitasking

Multitasking while attempting to listen is an excellent example of not being mentally or physically ready or emotionally available to listen. Obviously, there are times when the demands of life make multitasking unavoidable. However, many (if not most) of us easily fall into the habit of attempting of pay attention to too many things at once. Consequently, we spread our attention too thin and can't attend well to any of them.

Listening while multitasking isn't listening at all. It tells the other person that you're not really interested in listening and conveys the message that he or she isn't important enough for you to make yourself fully available. Each time your children have this experience, it is a micro-emotional rejection, a mini abandonment. While individual instances of this are no big deal in and of themselves, such experiences accumulate in the lives of your children and create serious ripple effects.

When this seeming lack of interest and availability becomes a pattern, children unconsciously internalize the message that you don't care enough about them to make listening to them a priority—they learn that they are unworthy of your attention. They effectively learn that they are unimportant, and this diminishes their self-esteem and sense of self in ways that can be long lasting.

Listening in the Face of Strong Emotions

Many people are uncomfortable in the presence of others' intense emotions, making it hard for them to listen. It's not unusual for powerful feelings such as fear, anger, sadness, and other forms of emotional pain to tap into the listener's past or present experiences in ways that evoke significant upset. Often, listeners are uncomfortable because they have no idea how to respond.

The most difficult pain for us to bear is that of those we care about the most. We feel as much (if not more) pain seeing our loved ones—especially our children—in pain. It can be anxiety provoking, stressful, and overwhelming. Difficulty tolerating our own discomfort can precipitate impulsive, unconscious reactions to try to fix our children's pain or avoid it.

As parents in recovery, we need to keep in mind how well versed we were in ways to avoid physical and emotional pain during our active addiction. Yet, as good as we may have been at escaping from and numbing our pain, we could never outrun it. It always caught up with us, coming back to bite us in the ass. And when it did, the pain was even worse. That's the way it is with discomfort and pain— avoidance strategies may work for a while, but ultimately they only amplify and extend the distress.

As much as you may want to take away your children's pain, you can't. If you practice twelve-step recovery and have worked Step One, you have experience accepting being powerless over your addiction. The recognition and acceptance of your limitations when your children are in physical or emotional pain is an extension of the work of Step One. In the same way that trying to control your active addiction created even more unmanageability in your life, attempting to exert control over your children's pain will only lead to unmanageability, magnifying and prolonging the pain for everyone involved. What you can do is be present with and for them when they are in pain and need to express it. This is no small task. It takes strength and courage to listen to and be present with the pain of your children.

8

CONNECTION THROUGH COMMUNICATION: PART II

If you light a lantern for another, it will also brighten your own way.

Nichiren

Although most of us are born with the physical ability to hear, listening is a process that requires our conscious attention and active participation, beginning with honoring the preconditions for listening. The preconditions for listening consist of setting the conscious intention to listen, making the commitment to listen, being mentally and physically ready to listen, and having willingness to allow the other person to complete their message. Being mindful of your thoughts and emotions helps lay the foundation for attuned active listening.

Ingredients for Active Listening

Active listening has several component parts, beginning with making the commitment to listen. The commitment to listen involves making yourself emotionally available and investing the time and energy needed to listen attentively.

This commitment is evidenced by such actions as turning toward the speaker and making eye contact, turning off the TV, putting down the smartphone, letting incoming calls go to voicemail (unless you're expecting an urgent call), turning away from the computer, temporarily discontinuing whatever else consumes your attention, and keeping other distractions at bay.

Being consciously present—physically and emotionally: There are myriad ways to demonstrate being present: physically orienting toward and giving your children your undivided attention in a non-judgmental way, holding their hand or placing your hand gently on their shoulder or knee as they relate a painful experience, neither being overwhelmed by nor needing to shrink from their pain, and listening with your heart when your child describes their day at school or with extracurricular activities

- **Quieting the mind:** Part of being consciously present, quieting the mind involves the application of basic mindfulness practice to simply notice and observe your thoughts and feelings, acknowledging them without becoming attached to them or striving to avoid them. When we quiet our mind, our listening becomes sharper and clearer, deeper and more perceptive. This facilitates the ability to listen with our heart as well as our ears.

- **Acknowledging:** Providing feedback in the form of words (verbal) and/or gestures (nonverbal) indicates an accurate reception of the message sent.

- **Encouraging:** Using verbal and nonverbal cues invites the other person to continue speaking.

- **Clarifying:** Using questions to request more information reduces potential confusion.

The following communications skills are actually basic counseling skills. However, anyone can learn and practice them to improve their ability to communicate with others, including their children.

Encouraging

In the context of active listening, encouraging has nothing to do with giving pep talks or patting your kids on the back, but rather prompting them to continue talking. Encouraging takes several verbal and nonverbal forms:

- nonverbal minimal responses, such as a nod of the head or engaged facial expressions

- verbal minimal responses, such as "Uh-huh" and "I see"

- repeating back the last two or three words your child says

- brief invitations to continue, such as "Go on" and "Tell me more"

By encouraging your children to keep talking, you indicate your continuing interest in what they have to say (and underneath that, your continuing interest in them—period). This strengthens the communication process and the connection between you.

Asking Questions with Intention

Asking questions in response to what your children tell you demonstrates that you are paying attention and are interested. Moreover, the strategic use of questions (and the answers they elicit) can help provide important clarification and increased understanding for both you and your children. However, be mindful not to barrage your kids with or overuse questions. It's a conversation, not an interrogation. Use questions to

- move from the general to the specific: "Your visit to the museum was 'good'? What in particular was good about it?"

- gather additional information and separate essential facts and feelings from side issues: "What was it about how your friend acted that you feel sad about?"

- ask for clarification when you are unclear about what your child said: "I'm not sure I understand. Can you please tell me more about what your teacher said?"

There are three fundamental types of questions:

- **Closed questions:** usually yield limited responses confined to "yes" or "no" answers and are the least helpful: "Was your day at school good or bad?"

- **Leading questions:** implicitly directive, leaning toward a particular answer or outcome: "Did you have a good day at school?"

- **Open questions:** invite a more complete and detailed response, encourage the speaker to continue talking, and are the most helpful: "How was your day at school?"

What if questions are a type of open question that can help the other person look at possibilities, including the potential results of alternative actions. "What do you think would happen if the next time you play basketball you wear sneakers instead of the hiking boots you wore today?" or "How do you think things might have been different if instead of continuing to argue with your cousin, you said, 'Let's just agree to disagree'?"

It's always more helpful to ask questions that begin with *how* or *what* rather than *why*. *How* and *what* focus on the process related to the other person's experience, whereas *why* often feels accusatory and leads to defensiveness. Posing the question "Why didn't you clean up after yourself in the kitchen?" invites evasiveness, excuses, defensiveness, and the always popular (and for parents, exasperating) "I don't know," when what you're really interested in is getting the kitchen clean.

Much more helpful are questions for this situation would be "What kept you from being able to clean up after yourself in the kitchen?" or "How can we make sure this gets done?" or "What can I do to help?" These are much more likely to create connection and lead to the desired behavior.

Reflecting Feelings

Reflecting feelings is a skill that focuses on identifying and clarifying the speaker's emotions and reflecting back that understanding with an empathetic tone. This is much more than simply repeating or paraphrasing what your children stated. It is about tuning in to how they *feel* and empathizing with those feelings. Reflective listening involves identifying the primary feelings the speaker is having.

With an accurate and empathic understanding of your children's feelings, you can better appreciate how an event or issue may be affecting them. For example, when listening to your child describe being rejected by other kids on the playground with what appears to be underlying hurt and sadness, you could reflect the feeling by saying, "It sounds like that experience hurt your feelings, and you felt sad."

When you successfully use the skill of reflecting feelings, it

- facilitates the expression of your children's emotions;

- generates feelings of expansive understanding and connection between you and your children;

- gives your children the experience of feeling "heard" at depth;

- lays the groundwork to help your children work through situations in which they are "stuck";

- lets your children know it's safe to share uncomfortable or painful feelings with you.

The following is another example of how to reflect your child's feelings.

Child: "If that jerk Sam hogs the ball the next time we play after school, I'm going to curse him out!"

Parent: "It sounds like you're really angry at him."

Child: "You bet I am! He needs to pass to me more. I'm better than he is, and we lost because he took so many shots."

Parent: "It's frustrating when you know you can do more to help your team."

Validating

Validation is the recognition *and* acceptance of another person's thoughts, feelings, and experiences as natural and normal, given the context in which they occurred. This is a skill that conveys powerful messages: *Your feelings make sense, and I understand why you feel the way you do. You are not bad or wrong or crazy for feeling the way you do.*

Accepting and validating your children's emotional reactions in no way means you agree with their behavior. Although feelings and actions are often closely related in that feelings frequently fuel action, emotions and behavior—how we feel versus how we act—are entirely different things. The feelings may be entirely natural and understandable, while the associated behavior is unacceptable. Differentiating between feelings and actions is part of the process of validation.

To understand why people (particularly children) need validation within the communication process, we need to consider how few places support the expression of strong emotions. Twelve-step recovery meetings and psychotherapy or counseling sessions are among the select environments where people can freely share intense feelings without experiencing judgment, shame, or being shut down. In our society, neighborhoods, and families, we often learn, for example, that strength means not crying, bravery means not feeling fear, and maturity equals never being angry or upset. Most of us have been subjected to an assortment of messages to the effect that our feelings are "wrong."

Showing strong emotion can make people extremely uncomfortable, which can drive efforts to avoid intense feeling by stemming its flow as quickly as possible. Frequently, this takes the form of trying to convince someone that his or her feelings are somehow inappropriate or otherwise not okay: "You shouldn't feel that way." As noted earlier, this is among the most unhelpful things you can say to anyone, especially your children.

Discomfort in the face of strong emotion and the need to squelch it can also assume the guise of impulsive and superficial attempts to reassure: "Don't worry. Everything will be okay." Even when your intent is to help your child feel better, acting under the influence of your own discomfort with his or her emotional pain may inadvertently send the message that it's not okay for your child to feel badly.

In order to skillfully validate your children's feelings, you need to actually feel some aspect of what they feel. This empathic attunement doesn't mean you have to have the exact same feelings as your child or that your emotional response to the situation being discussed would be the same. What makes validation genuine is the willingness to connect with and draw from your own experience to connect with the emotion your child expresses.

The skills of reflecting and validating feelings are simple to describe but difficult to master. However, learning how to use them doesn't require an advanced degree or specialized training but rather the application of conscious awareness and practice. These skills involve learning how to meta-listen: to listen with your heart, in addition to your head, in order to hear the messages beneath the spoken words.

Whatever else your children may be saying when they express their feelings, they are indirectly asking, "Are my feelings okay?" "Can you handle them?" By extension, they are also asking, "Am I okay?" "Can you handle me?" "Will you accept me?" When we can listen to and accept our children's intense emotions—anger, fear, sadness, remorse/guilt, ambivalence, etc.—without turning away or shutting them down, we show them a powerful form of acceptance that resonates both consciously and unconsciously. It is a manifestation of unconditional love.

Speaking so Your Kids Will Listen

Speaking to our children tends to come much more easily and naturally than listening to them. This section focuses on awareness and skills of speaking with your kids to facilitate connection. Part of our job as parents is to guide our children through the maze of life. We are responsible for taking care of them from birth until whenever. They are supposed to listen to us—especially when we talk (dammit). Reality, of course, loves to rear its ugly head and laugh at us.

It's easy to fall into the pattern of talking *at* our kids, but turning conversations with your children into monologues rarely helps. Consider how you felt when your parent(s) resorted to lecturing, making speeches, or giving sermons when talking with you. Unless you want your children to tune out you and what you say, resist the urge to lecture them as much as you can. This is especially important if you're operating under the influence of strong or heated emotions. As 19th century American writer Ambrose Bierce admonished, "Speak when you are angry and you will make the best speech you will ever regret." As a parent, I've had the experience of being carried away by the force of my upset, followed immediately by feelings of remorse, more often than I care to admit.

There is a world of difference between talking *at* your kids and talking *with* them. While there are times when it's important for you to talk and for your children to listen, communication with your kids—whether they are eight or eighteen—works best when it takes the form of a dialogue—an exchange of ideas, opinions, or perspectives, a give-and-take between two or more people who take turns speaking and listening.

Being consciously present and quieting the mind were described earlier as active listening skills, but bringing them to bear when speaking to your kids is also of tremendous benefit. If you have carry-over stress, irritability, agitation, or upset from work, relationships, or other sources, the more you can be aware of it and intentionally set it aside, the more you will be able to be present-centered and emotionally available when you engage your kids in conversation.

When you speak, try to be conscious of pausing between sentences, even briefly. This will give your children time to process what you're saying (believe it or not) and improve their level of understanding. Such spaces between statements also provide you with a valuable opportunity to take a step back as necessary and modulate the tone and volume of your voice.

The extent to which the attention of kids (especially that of young children but also teenagers) can wander is impressive. Sometimes it's unintentional, and other times they simply don't care to hear what you're saying. When my daughters were young and it was apparent that they weren't listening when I needed to speak to them, I found it helpful to ask them for eye contact: "Please look at me." "Let me see your eyes." "I need to see some eyes." After they became used to this scenario and I wanted their full attention, all I needed to say was "eyes," and they would make eye contact with me.

Ask your kids for their input to facilitate interaction and feedback: "Does what I'm saying make sense?" "What do you think?" "Do you have any questions?" These questions create dialogue and send the message that you welcome their input and respect their opinion. Demonstrating to your children that their views are important to you has great therapeutic value in and of itself. It empowers them and enhances their self-esteem.

That is not to say that you will always agree with their opinions—obviously, you won't. Healthy communication has space for divergent perspectives, even if some of those perspectives come from children rather than adults. The key is to express those disagreements respectfully (though obviously, as necessary and appropriate, the parent's position is the one that needs to hold sway). As the literature of my twelve-step program suggests, "We can disagree without being disagreeable."

When you need to give your kids constructive criticism on their behavior, using "I" statements will make it less likely that they'll experience it as an attack and become defensive. The point at which either party in a conversation gets defensive is usually the place where connection and any real communication stop. "I" statements, such as the following, will help your children see things from your perspective: "I get very frustrated when I ask you to clean your room and you don't do it." "I get angry when I've asked you to clean your room two or three times and I come home from work and it still isn't done."

It's important to be aware of your nonverbal behavior—body language, gestures, facial expression, tone of voice/inflection, and voice volume. As the thirteenth century Persian poet Rumi expressed so elegantly, "Raise your words, not voice. It is rain that grows flowers, not thunder." Frowning disapprovingly, manifesting impatience with a sharp edge to your voice, or using sarcasm (as understandable as these behaviors may be under certain circumstances) while speaking with your children leaves them feeling judged, put-down, and not good enough. Such emotional rejections invariably bruise their sense of self.

This is not to say that you need to tip-toe delicately when speaking with your children, far from it. Rather, the aim is to help you attain the awareness and resources to be the most skillful communicator you can be.

With my own (now adult) children, I set my intention to spend more time listening and less time talking. There are times when I actualize this intention quite well and others when I fall short. Naturally, I want to share the wisdom of my experience with them as much as possible. And whenever they say things that are (in my sometimes not-so-humble opinion) incorrect or that might lead them down what I believe to be an unhelpful path, I still have the impulse to correct them or give advice with the belief that they should listen to me (dammit!). However, through practice I've learned to mobilize enough conscious awareness to observe these thoughts and let go of my attachment to the need to direct my daughters. I no longer hold on to the need to be "right" as if it's a priceless gem.

I try to practice a framework with Buddhist origins, which I've heard paraphrased in the rooms of twelve-step recovery, and remember to ask myself:

- Is what I have in mind to say true?

- Is it necessary?

- Is it necessary that I say it now?

- Can I say it with kindness?

If the answer to these questions isn't yes, it gives me pause to consciously consider whether what I was going to say is better left unsaid. Increasingly, I leave more unsaid.

During conversations with my daughters, whether in person or via phone, I frequently ask, "Is there anything I can do to be helpful?" Usually, the answer is some version of "No, but thank you for asking." Through that one question, I convey the message—consciously and unconsciously—that I am here for them, the antithesis of codependent approval-seeking or a need to be needed. For me, it is part of my ongoing living amends as well as an embodiment of service. Ultimately, it always comes back to being present with them.

Before each conversation concludes, I make it a point to tell my daughters that I love them. Often they say it back but not always. And that's okay. I say "I love you" because it's my truth (even when there is some sort of conflict or disagreement between us), and even if they know it, I want to make certain they hear it in the moment. I've learned and become better at applying the wisdom of trading off what I may want for a deeper sense of connection and emotionally availability steeped in love.

And we are all better for it.

9

RECONCILING LOVE
AND LIMITS

*Whenever you're in conflict with someone,
there is one factor that can make the difference between
damaging your relationship and deepening it.*

That factor is attitude.

William James

Oscillating between maddening, anxiety-provoking, terrifying, gratifying, rewarding, and beautiful beyond description, parenting is an amazing adventure. As wonderful as children can be and frequently are, they can (and often do) act in ways that are absolutely crazy making. Just doing what comes naturally to them—essentially what they are "supposed" to do consistent with their age (whether two, six, nine, thirteen, sixteen, etc.) and developmental stage—

they are sometimes the world's most effective advertisements for birth control.

Getting them to listen and comply with our requests can be an exhausting exercise in frustration. There are times when we have to ask or tell them over and over (and over) again to do something— clean up after themselves, do their homework, say "please" when they want something and "thank you" when they're given something, feed the dog or the cat—and they still don't do it. At other times, we earnestly ask or tell them to *stop* doing something—yelling for you at the top of their lungs from a different part of your home when they need your assistance, teasing and antagonizing their siblings, leaving windows or doors open when the air conditioning is on, paying more attention to their smartphone than to you when you're talking to them—and they continue to do it, time after time.

Parents struggle mightily to understand such stunning noncompliance. Is it a lack of caring, utter indifference, willful opposition, or an inability to follow through? The most useful answer may be one proposed by an old-school comedian, who described this phenomenon as the inherent "brain damage" of childhood.

Kids Have a Developmental Need for Structure and Limits

Believe it or not, children desire structure, though this typically operates unconsciously, underneath the surface of their awareness. They thrive in home environments where there's a healthy balance between freedom to be who they are and limits to behaving in ways that are unhealthy and/or unsafe. Children need their parents to set and enforce limits. Psychologically, they need their parents to be in control in order for them to feel safe emotionally.

In this context, control doesn't mean the internal need to control people and situations in order to create the preferred outcomes described in previous chapters. Rather, I'm referring to appropriate leadership, oversight, and governance of the family and household. Parents need to be in charge, not the kids. Moreover, kids need to know that their parents are in charge and have their shit together when it comes to being in charge.

Of course, kids usually don't like the limits set for them and often push back against them or even fight them, especially as they get older. But without limits—or with limits that aren't enforced—children are beyond their parents' appropriate control or effectively out of control. While they may seem to revel in this "freedom" and say how much they prefer it, it comes at a cost. Children may not be consciously aware of it, and older children (teenagers especially) will deny it, but deep down they feel unsafe and uncared for when their parents don't set limits on them and they are effectively allowed to do what they want whenever they want.

Providing structure and limits is one way in which parents take care of their children. Setting and enforcing limits means that parents love their children enough to risk upset and anger. It demonstrates that parents have the ability to withstand and "hold" their children's reactions of emotional upset; even when these reactions are related to parental actions, they contribute to increased unconscious feelings of safety for children.

Setting and enforcing limits; implementing appropriate and healthy boundaries; determining which "battles" are worth fighting; minimizing getting involved in power struggles; identifying, applying, and implementing logical consequences without shaming; and distinguishing consequences from punishment are all skills that can be learned and practiced. And applying the mindfulness practices of observing, accepting, and regulating your thoughts and emotions as well as the communication skills described in previous chapters will enable you to set and enforce limits with your kids more skillfully and successfully.

We naturally want our children to comply with our wishes, and feel frustrated, angry, and perhaps disappointed and hurt when they don't do as we ask. Children want their parents to back off. They feel put upon, pressured, or controlled. Ultimately, both parents and their kids want to be heard. However, when we engage in power struggles with our children as if it's a zero-sum scenario and we hold out to win against our children, someone always loses—usually everyone. We need to empathize with the pressures, stresses, and life challenges they're experiencing.

The Therapeutic Value of Saying No

There is a Grand Canyon-sized chasm between being empathic and overly permissive. Parents do their children a tremendous disservice when they don't give them the experience of being told no.

For many parents, it's consistently enticing to say yes to their children's wishes, particularly if they can afford to gratify those wishes but often even if they really can't. Parents naturally want their kids to be happy. However, the happiness provided by material things is fleeting at best, and research shows there's a deviation-amplifying side to needing to have the next new "thing," be it the must-have toy of the moment or the new smartphone model others have. It fosters a sense of deficiency that can only be sated temporarily.[15]

Your kids may be extremely grateful when they first receive the new "hot" item, but all too frequently that fades to black as soon as the next new hotness hits the market. At that point, in the minds of such kids, what they have is quickly rendered obsolete and deeply unsatisfying. And, if you give in and get your kids that newest hotness, when the next iteration becomes available, the dynamic is repeated. This becomes an ongoing vicious circle that creates unhappiness and dissatisfaction. Among the most valuable lessons you can teach your kids is that genuine happiness isn't found in getting what you want; it's embedded in appreciating and making the most of what you have.

Learning how to deal with not getting what you want and when you want it is an essential skill that everyone needs to develop. Many parents are loath to set and enforce limits with their kids because they don't want to be subjected to their kids' upset, because they have an unhealthy desire to be friends with their kids, want their kids to have everything they want or to have more than they did as

---

15 Scott Sonenshein, "To Raise Better Kids, Say No," *New York Times* (May 17, 2017) https://www.nytimes.com/2017/05/17/well/family/to-raise-better-kids-say-no.html?smid=fb-share&_r=0.

children, or don't want their kids to be deprived as they may have been. Do any of these resonate with you?

Even for parents who, for whatever reason, do everything they can to avoid saying no to their kids, there will inevitably come a point when they want to and must impose limits. This will be a new form of hell for all involved. When your children are accustomed to being overindulged, not getting whatever they want feels to them like deprivation. As a Chinese proverb puts it, "Parents who are afraid to put their foot down usually have children who step on their toes."

Saying no is a form of setting limits. Naturally, your kids will test the limits you set and test you to confirm whether or not the limit is real. They may beg, plead, whine, cry, tantrum up a storm, get extremely angry, or all of the above. Partly this reflects their distress at not getting what they want, but they also want to see if they can get you to give in. If you give in, you send the message to your kids that "no" doesn't necessarily mean no, and that if they beg, plead, whine, or cry, they'll get what they want. Giving in reinforces your kids' cringe-inducing behavior, making it more likely to recur and more difficult to extinguish.

The slipperiness of this slope can't be overstated. If you are firm and hold to the limits you set consistently, your kids will progressively learn to accept those limits much more easily and quickly. On the other hand, if you hold firm initially, your kids wear you down and get you to give in by continuing to beg, plead, whine, or cry, but in essence, what you've taught them is that if they just beg, plead, whine, or cry long enough, eventually they'll get what they want.

When you say no, there needn't be a lot of drama. Being straightforward and steadfast while injecting a touch of lighthearted humor can make this process relatively painless. My daughters' mother and I routinely used the phrases "Get real, Neil," "No way, Jose," "No chance, Lance," and "Nope, not happening." We repeated these responses matter-of-factly as necessary—like a mantra or a song stuck on repeat—and it proved extremely successful in helping our daughters learn to accept that, in those cases, they weren't going to get what they wanted.

If there are two (or more) parents involved, obviously it's critical for them to be in agreement when it comes to setting and enforcing limits. Conflict between parents usually causes them to undermine each other and sends mixed and confusing messages to their kids. Also kids who are adept at learning how to play one parent against the other, figure out which parent to go to in order to maximize the chances of getting what they want. This area becomes more complex when the parents aren't together, but it's in the best interests of their kids for their parents to strive to sing from the same sheet of music to the maximum extent they can.

Children need structure and limits, and parents need to have the courage and strength to risk and withstand the emotional onslaught of their children's frustration, sadness, anger, and other forms of upset. This is a form of distress tolerance and can be incredibly difficult for many parents. I don't know any parent who enjoys it when their kids are angry at them, but if you continually give in to your children's wishes and desires, doing whatever they want and getting them whatever they want, it creates an unrealistic expectation of how the world works. They learn to see the world as existing to serve their perceived needs, making it harder for them to be successful in the future, under circumstances indifferent to those needs.

Children need to have the experience of learning how to delay gratification and cope with the limits placed upon them. Mindfulness practices can be an instrumental part of this learning process. The resilience your children develop from such experiences lasts a lifetime, whereas the anger and upset they direct at you is only temporary.

Styles of Parenting

Generally, parents exhibit one of four principal styles of parenting—authoritarian, permissive/overindulgent, uninvolved, and authoritative—although some parents may exhibit characteristics of other styles as well.

Authoritarian

Authoritarian parents are strict and controlling. They expect children to follow a rigid set of rules and expectations and generally rely on punishment to teach a lesson. They place a high priority on obedience and use punishment as a means of getting their children to do what they ask. They allow for little open dialogue between parent and child—little input from their children is sought or allowed.

Authoritarian parents rank low in responsiveness to their children's needs and desires and are reserved in the amount of warmth and nurturing they show their children, placing a higher value on conformity and compliance. Parents with this style tend to have strict rules they believe should be followed no matter what and rarely provide explanations for the rules other than "Because I said so."

Permissive/Overindulgent

Warm and accepting, these parents are often overly lenient and avoid confrontation with their kids. Permissive parents rank high in responsiveness to their children's whims but low in requiring accountability from them. They set few limits and have few rules for their children, and those that do exist are enforced only inconsistently and are often compromised to accommodate the child's mood and wishes. Negotiations with the children replace parental limits.

The sense from these parents is "I wish you wouldn't, but okay, if that's what you want." Such parents will bribe their children with rewards to get them to do what they want. The kids may have the final say in family decisions, and adolescents are often viewed as mini-adults. Permissive parents often rescue their children from experiencing the natural consequences of their behavior.

Uninvolved

Parents with this style may be so uninvolved that they actually neglect their children and their needs. Uninvolved parents rank low in responsiveness to their children's needs *and* in requiring accountability. They often appear indifferent to or know very little about what's going on in the lives of their children. They present as distracted, cold, even rejecting.

Such parents are emotionally unavailable to their children and frequently absent physically. They provide few rules and fewer consequences. Uninvolved parents often defer decision-making or pay little attention to the child's response when making a decision. They tend to rely on teachers, coaches, or social service and juvenile justice resources to manage their child's growth and well-being. The underlying message is "Do what you want. I don't care."

Authoritative

Authoritative parents set realistic limits and require their children to adhere to them. Firm but fair, they provide warmth, affection, and mutual respect. The children know the ultimate authority resides with the parent. Parents with this style ensure their children have structure that includes planned bedtimes and clear household rules.

Authoritative parents have reasonable, age-appropriate expectations of their children, and the children understand these expectations. Children receive both logical and natural consequences for rule violations and misbehaviors. These parents are emotionally available to their children, and there is open communication in which children feel safe in talking with their parents without fear of harsh judgment or criticism. The underlying message is "I love you unconditionally, but there are conditions on our relationship." Authoritative parenting is widely regarded as the most effective and mutually beneficial style of parenting.

Ultimately, the reality that parents are in charge must be unambiguous. Healthy child development requires the respective roles of parents and children to be crystal clear while providing appropriate space for open communication. Parents are responsible for providing healthy structure, including well-defined boundaries and limits. That notwithstanding, they also need to endeavor to create age-appropriate opportunities for mutual decision-making and even power sharing with their children.

Assign Your Children Chores

Even young children are perfectly capable of helping around the house; giving them chores is both helpful and healthy—the earlier, the better, as long as they are developmental stage-appropriate chores. For example, with parental guidance and expectation, younger children can learn to put away their toys and clear their dishes from the table after meals. Show them how to do new chores you assign, and do the chores with them the first few times until they get the hang of it. Then give them the responsibility to do the chores on their own.

If (or, more likely, when) they have questions or need further guidance, be available to provide it, but actually completing the chores is on your kids. Chores teach your kids that you're not there to do everything for them, including clean up after them. Assigning chores creates the understanding that your kids need to contribute to their environment by giving them specific responsibilities to actualize it.

Proactive Positive Attention

In the same way that the best time to pay attention to your health is when you are healthy, the best time to pay attention to your kids is when they don't require it.

Let your children know when they've done something positive, helpful, or healthy. Children naturally seek their parents' approval but unconsciously follow the psychological aphorism that negative attention is better than no attention, and when Mom or Dad focuses more on frustrating or annoying behaviors (as parents often do), that can be a powerful motivator for their children's behavior. As a countermeasure, strive to "catch" your kids behaving well. Practice actively looking for demonstrations of positive behavior on their part, and you will be more likely to notice when your kids behave well. When you do, tell them, and show your approval.

In whitewater rafting, guides recommended that you focus your attention not on the rocks you want to avoid but on the open water where you want to go. This doesn't mean you only see what you want to see or that you avoid paying necessary attention to those rocks and other potential hazards, but what we focus our attention on becomes larger in our awareness. Proactively looking for opportunities to give your kids positive attention enlarges your awareness of what they do that's positive. Whenever your kids shift their behavior in a positive direction (meeting your expectations, adhering to your rules, respecting the limits you've set, etc.), let them know that you recognize their efforts and express appreciation. Some parents believe praising their kids for doing what they've asked is unnecessary, but if you want to guide their behavior, providing positive reinforcement always helps.

Praise is most helpful when given in proportion to the action being praised. Over-the-top, disproportionately effusive praise risks feeding kids' narcissism and sense of entitlement. After all, they helped out around the house; it's not as though they solved homelessness. Tell your kids specifically what they did that you liked. For example, "Thank you for cleaning your room," or "I appreciate it when you include your sister." Let your kids know that you recognize their efforts and actions with a pat on the back, a hand on their shoulder, or a hug. Do something with your kids that they like to do, such as playing a game, reading a story, or going for a walk.

Providing Structured Choices

The opportunity to make choices is important because it gives children a sense that they have some influence on their surroundings and what happens to them, contributing to a sense of competence and self-efficacy. Providing opportunities for choice gives kids a sense of empowerment through the act of choosing. Even young children engaged in exploring and gaining a sense of their own autonomy need appropriate opportunities to assert themselves.

As an alternative to giving directions or commands, parents can offer their children *structured choices*—choices between acceptable predetermined options. When asking children to do things they will likely oppose, such as brushing their teeth or doing their homework, structured choices can engage their cooperation. This facilitates the win-win scenario in which your kids do what you need them to do, while they exercise a measure of autonomy through personal choice.

The choices you can offer your kids include *what* they obtain through their behavior, *when* they do certain things, *with whom* they interact, and *how* they accomplish activities. Structured choices allow children to choose between two or more options, for example, what clothes they wear, what they eat, how and with what they play, in what activities they can engage, the order in which necessary tasks are completed, and when and with whom to complete those tasks.

All children can benefit from being offered structured choices, but the options within those choices must be age appropriate. Children under the age of five need simple choices along the lines of "You have a choice—you can wear the blue shirt or the black shirt," or "You have a choice—you can color or play with your blocks."

Intentional structured choices give kids the structure they need, while allowing them to practice decision making. Other examples include:

- "Would you like to brush your teeth before or after your bedtime story?

- "Would you prefer carrots, zucchini, or broccoli with dinner?"

- "Do you want to do your homework before or after your hour of video games?"

- "Do you want to clean your room when you get home from school or after dinner?"

- "You can turn down the volume on the music or put on your headphones."

As your children get older, they can increasingly participate in a dialogue about and potentially have input in setting rules, expectations, and consequences. However, the bottom line is that these remain parental decisions, and *you* are the ultimate arbiter and have the final say.

It's important to understand the difference between a structured choice and a choice between compliance and consequences. The former involves two (or more) acceptable or preapproved options. In contrast, the latter indicates one acceptable course of behavior along with the negative consequences of misbehavior. For example, "You can mow the grass today or be grounded tonight" *is* a choice, but a very different type of choice.

Setting and Enforcing Limits

Setting limits for your kids involves letting them know what behavior is and is not acceptable. This includes the expectations you have and the rules you establish for your children. Enforcing limits is about the actions parents take when children don't meet those expectations or violate the rules. In order to be effective in guiding your kids toward acceptable behavior, these actions we take to enforce limits often need to include consequences. Although it may be counterintuitive for many parents, limits *can* be set with love and enforced with kindness.

If you practice twelve-step recovery, you've likely heard the saying, "You can make any choice you want as long as you're willing to accept the consequences of that choice." A consequence is a result of something a person does. By allowing children to experience the consequences of their behavior—both positive and painful—parents help their kids learn what happens as a result of the choices they make and the actions they take. The consequences of their actions help teach kids to be responsible and accountable.

You may be wondering, what's the difference between a consequence and punishment? A consequence is a result or effect of an action or condition. In contrast, a punishment is the imposition of a penalty as retribution for an offense. How you communicate a set limit to your kids, in combination with your attitude and the spirit in which you enforce the limit, determines whether the outcome is a consequence or a punishment. The most fundamental difference between a consequence and a punishment lies in the intention and implementation.

We can't make our children understand messages they aren't ready to receive, but we can parent in ways that increase their readiness and capacity to receive them. And aspects of conscious awareness and intentional action can help parents achieve that goal.

It's normal for children to oppose rules and expectations.

Expect it to happen because it will. Ideally, your kids will respect your rules and limits, making the need to enforce those limits by imposing consequences rare. But realistically, even the most well-behaved kids need consequences at times. Testing limits is a natural part of children's learning process, so often they'll do whatever you tell them *not* to do just to see what happens and to see if you truly mean what you say. Remember, children learn more from what their parents do than from what they say. Try not to take your kids' limit-testing and other misbehaviors personally.

Clear messages are essential.

Keep it simple and be clear as to what the expectations, rules, and limits are. Tell your kids specifically what you want them to do. The expectations you create, the rules you lay down, and the limits you set for your kids need to be realistic and achievable, consistent with their age and abilities. Otherwise, you're setting up a no-win situation destined to cause suffering for them and you. Moreover, rules and limits need to be measurable so both you and your kids know with certainty whether or not the expectation has been met, the rule followed, or the limit adhered to.

If you intend to impose a consequence for an infraction, specify in advance what that consequence will be. Confirm that your kids understand the expectation and the potential consequence by having them repeat it back to you.

Construct consequences with conscious intention.

Consequences for misbehavior are part of the structure that helps teach children responsibility and accountability. They can help kids develop the skills of self-management, but to serve this purpose well, consequences need to be thoughtful. Well-formed consequences are immediate, logical, and proportionate.

Immediate: Consequences need to follow the unacceptable behavior as soon as possible. Allowing days to elapse between your kids' misbehavior and implementing the consequences for it dilutes their meaning and value as a learning tool and can be confusing to your kids. Taking some time—ideally a day or less—to formulate an appropriate logical and proportionate consequence is fine.

Logical: Consequences are most beneficial when they are closely connected to the misbehavior—the more direct the connection the better. This provides your kids with a clear connection between their behavior and the consequence. For example, your young child continues to ride his bike after you asked him several times to put it away and come inside. The logical consequence? Take his bike away for a specific amount of time. Similarly, your teenage daughter comes home at 10:30 p.m. when her curfew was 9:30 p.m.; no extraordinary circumstances justify it, and this has happened more than once. The logical consequence is an earlier curfew for a specified period. Or if your daughter makes a mess in the kitchen while making something to eat and, contrary to the rules you've established, doesn't clean it up, the logical consequence involves cleaning the kitchen for a specified period.

You may have heard the term "natural consequences" and wondered how they are different from logical consequences. Natural consequences are the inevitable result of a child's own actions. For example, despite your strong suggestion, your son doesn't reapply sunscreen during a day at the beach. The natural consequence is that he gets a nasty and painful sunburn. Natural consequences can occur without parental involvement, whereas logical consequences are imposed by a parent or caregiver.

Proportionate: Consequences need to be enough to reinforce the limit set and teach your kids the necessary lesson but without being too harsh, too much, or too long. There should be a direct correlation between the seriousness of the misbehavior and the severity of the consequence. In other words, less serious rule violations should have smaller consequences. For example, first infractions should also result in less severe consequences, but subsequent violations of the same rule appropriately deserve larger consequences.

Using the previous examples once again, if your young child continues to ride his bike after you asked him several times to put his bike away and come inside, a proportionate consequence would be to take his bike away for a day. For your teenage daughter who came home at 10:30 p.m. when her curfew was 9:30 p.m., a proportionate consequence would require her to come home at 8:30 p.m. the following night. For your daughter who made a mess in the kitchen and didn't clean up after herself, the proportionate consequence would be to wash all the dinner dishes or perhaps clean the entire kitchen.

Implement consequences with care.

Focus on the problematic behavior, not the child. Messages that blame, criticize non-constructively, or shame are unhelpful and often backfire, fueling anger that children then act out by becoming more oppositional and blowing off more rules and limits. Messages like "You're so self-centered!" "You never think about anyone else!" or "How many times have I asked you to clean up after yourself?" will likely generate resentment.

Be specific to the issue at hand. If the specific incident is part of a clear pattern, reflect that observation. It's never helpful to overgeneralize by using the words *never* and *always*, such as "You *never* put your bike away." "You *always* come home after your curfew."

When giving consequences to your kids it's important to be matter-of-fact in your manner, tone of voice, and voice volume. Mindfulness can make a significant, positive difference here. Take enough time to tune in to and observe your thoughts and emotions, and self-calm so you can respond intentionally rather than react reflexively out of frustration, anger, or hurt. Yelling in anger only makes everyone involved (including you) feel worse. Alternatively, if your kids see you've lost control, they may feel that they have somehow "won" and may be more likely to repeat the offending behavior and test other limits you set.

Imposing consequences doesn't have to be a big deal. The process can be straightforward and drama free without long explanations or further justifications. Arguing with your kids about the imposition of consequences can lead them to think they might get their way if they persist. Cut off arguments with simple, direct statements, such as "We're done talking about it."

And, although your kids may not like the outcome and might bitch and moan about it, the process doesn't have to be painful for them or for you. The firmer, clearer, and more business-as-usual you can be, the smoother the process will go and the more successful it will be in facilitating better behavior from your kids.

When a consequence ends, allow it to be over and done with. It's never helpful to lecture, nag, or continue to bring it up. Give your kids the opportunity to learn from the experience, adjust their behavior, and move on.

Be prepared to follow through.

Children learn to follow rules and respect limits when parents do what they say they are going to do if those rules and limits are ignored or violated. It's reasonable—and, in the case of newly set limits or established rules, appropriate—to give one or sometimes two warnings, but then you need to take action consistent with your words. Action means enforcing the limits you set by imposing consequences. This need not represent punishment—it's simply the consequence of not following the rules.

Never state a consequence with which you're not prepared to follow through. When you set a limit that your kids violate, and you don't follow through with the stated consequence, your kids learn that you don't necessarily mean what you say, and that consequences may well not follow rule infractions. Subsequently, they'll be less likely to respect the limits you set and more likely to test them further.

For example, "You need to put away your toys after you finish playing with them, and we've talked about this before. If you don't put them away today, you won't be able to play with them tomorrow." If they ignore or transgress this limit, and the parent doesn't take away those toys the next day, kids learn it is okay not to put their toys away. With older kids and teenagers, the rule might be about curfew. When you specify a curfew and your kids violate it, not enforcing that limit by imposing the stated consequence sends the message that it's not important and you're not really serious about it, making it much more likely they'll ignore curfew in the future.

Now, that being said, reasonable exceptions can and should be taken into consideration when enforcing limits and implementing consequences. However, these should be few and far between. When exceptions become common, they are no longer exceptions but standard procedure. Consistency is critical when it comes to setting and enforcing limits. Consistency means you do the same thing in the same situation and your actions align with your words.

The structure provided by setting limits helps cultivate the soil in which children grow healthy roots, and the accountability they learn when we enforce those limits helps them develop sturdy wings.

The Complications of Codependency

Parents inclined toward codependency can have additional challenges setting and enforcing limits. Codependency is a mode of relating to oneself and others defined by a pattern of excessively (and often obsessively) focusing on looking after and taking care of others at the expense of one's own needs. Although codependency is generally associated with families in which there is addiction, and is usually linked to the partners or parents of active addicts, it's a much more far-reaching issue. Increasingly, codependency is now believed to be a response to childhood trauma.

It's not unusual for people in recovery to struggle with codependency in ways that can impact how they parent their children. As my friend Bob S., who has been in recovery for over forty years, says, "Scratch an addict, and a codependent bleeds."

People who are codependent tend to have

1. difficulty determining where their responsibility appropriately ends and the responsibility of others begins. As a result, they have an exaggerated sense of responsibility for the actions of others;

2. a tendency to do more than their share much of the time;

3. a tendency to feel hurt when people don't recognize their efforts, including efforts no one requested;

4. an unhealthy dependence on relationships, sometimes going to extraordinary lengths to hold on to a relationship;

5. a fear of abandonment and of being alone;

6. a tendency to sacrifice their own needs to accommodate other people;

7. a sense of guilt when asserting themselves and their needs;

8. a need to control others, usually through manipulating, cajoling, promising, pleading, and bargaining;

9. difficulty saying no to others and setting limits.

A Word (or a Few) on Physical Discipline

Over the last five decades, attitudes in the United States about physical discipline, also known as corporal punishment, have evolved dramatically. Physical discipline in the forms of spanking, slapping, punching, kicking, and hitting children with objects of all sorts (belts and extension cords were especially popular) was once widely accepted. To a now disturbing extent, it was often encouraged and supported, based on the misguided belief, "Spare the rod and spoil the child." When I attended elementary school in the 1960s and early 1970s, teachers could hit students with impunity—and that was in public school!

Having had two children of my own, I know well the impulse to strike out at a child. I can't help but understand and empathize with it. There are circumstances when the apparent unwillingness of kids to listen to their parents is absolutely exasperating. When we want our kids to do something and they don't do it, especially when they ignore or blow off repeated requests (to clean up, turn off the TV, do their homework, brush their teeth, don't pull on the dog's fur or leave food on the table or mess with the remote control), the natural, consequent, emotional reactions are a mix of "You've got to be fucking kidding me," confusion, impatience, hurt, frustration, and anger. Yet, there is a world of difference between having the occasional natural and—I dare say—normal impulse to hit a child and acting out that impulse by actually doing it.

The only time I ever "hit" one of my daughters occurred when my eldest daughter was about two and a half years old. She picked up something from a shelf on a bookcase, and I told her to put it back. The fact that I can't even remember what she picked up shows just how inconsequential the item was. Although she understood my request, she refused to listen and held on to whatever it was.

Developmentally speaking, she simply did what a two-and-a-half year old child is supposed to do: test her independence during that first phase of the separation-individuation process (the second phase being adolescence), experiencing herself as her own person distinct from me and her mother. It was early in my clinical social work career, and although I had an intellectualized sense of this, I was tired and cranky and could feel my impatience and frustration rising. I asked her several times to put whatever the hell it was back on the shelf, but she continued to hold on to it. Finally, I grabbed it from her tiny, delicate hand and put it back myself.

I stood in stunned disbelief as she looked right at me, walked over to the shelf, and reached out her hand to pick up the item again. I sternly told her once, and then a second time, "Don't pick that up." By now, my anger was coiled like a rattlesnake, ready to strike. She went ahead and picked it up, looked directly at me, and started to smile. Chances were she thought we were playing some sort of game, but I automatically interpreted her actions as willful, unmitigated defiance that demanded a strong response. Impulsively, I smacked her hand—hard.

My guilt-laden regret was instantaneous. I watched in horror as the change in her demeanor seemed to start at her feet and work its way up her little body in slow motion until her smile dissolved into a frown, and her lips began to quiver. As she started to cry, she looked at me as if to say, "How could you do that to me? You're supposed to protect me." I felt as though I had betrayed her—because I had. I don't know if it was traumatic for her, but it was for me. Shortly thereafter, she didn't remember the experience. I, on the other hand, will never forget it.

Although there are holdouts that insist on reserving the so-called right to spank or otherwise physically discipline their kids, since approximately the 1980s, these activities have generally and appropriately been viewed as child abuse. Ample research demonstrates that physical punishments do kids considerably more harm than good.

The Report on Physical Punishment in the United States: What Research Tells Us about Its Effects on Children by Elizabeth T. Gershoff, PhD, addresses the association between parental physical punishment and eleven child behaviors and experiences. A meta-analytic and theoretical review of over one hundred years of social science research and hundreds of published studies on physical punishment, conducted by professionals in the fields of psychology, medicine, education, social work, and sociology, found that[16]

- there is little evidence that physical punishment improves children's behavior in the long term, and increasing empirical data indicates the physical punishment of children is an ineffective parenting practice;

- physical punishment makes it more, rather than less, likely that children will be defiant and aggressive in the future;

- physical punishment puts children at risk for a range of negative outcomes, including increased mental health problems;

- children who are physically punished are at greater risk of serious injury and physical abuse;

- when administered regularly, physical punishment increases antisocial behaviors such as lying, stealing, cheating, bullying, assaulting a sibling or peers, and lack of remorse for wrongdoing;

- physical punishment serves as a model for aggressive behavior and inappropriate ways of dealing with conflict;

- physical punishment erodes trust between a parent and child;

- adults who were hit frequently as children are more likely to suffer from depression and other negative social and mental health outcomes.

Dealing with Teenagers

It should come as no surprise that teenagers can present special challenges for parents. As noted earlier, the central developmental task of adolescence is to move toward becoming independent

---

16   E.T. Gershoff, *Report on Physical Punishment in the United States: What Research Tells Us About Its Effects on Children.* Columbus, OH: Center for Effective Discipline (2008).

while continuing to live at home. Separation-individuation requires teenagers to distance themselves from their parents psychologically in preparation to part from them physically. This process can be extremely difficult to negotiate for teens as well as their parents. But, with enhanced conscious awareness and mindful action, both you and your kids can weather the storm of adolescence and come out of it without capsizing.

Expect complaints.

Adolescents are supposed to be oppositional, rebellious, and moody, expressing dissent, disapproval, dissatisfaction, and resentment. Most parents naturally interpret this as ingratitude, though that's not necessarily the case at all. Teenage complaints are part of the process of separating and individuating. Just because your teenage kids complain frequently doesn't mean they lack gratitude for what you have done and continue to do for them. Conscious awareness of this supports your capacity for distress tolerance.

Be selective when picking your battles.

Be mindful in determining what to make an issue. When is it truly necessary, and when is it more about needing to be right or be in control? Make allowances for some oppositional attitude and behaviors that assert independence. Conflict with your teenagers will find you; you don't need to go looking for it.

Separation-individuation takes many forms that drive parents crazy but don't have to: from the infamous adolescent eye-roll, bottomless sighs, and sarcastic comments to the off-putting assortment of other nonverbal and semi-verbal responses when you ask questions or try to engage your teenagers in conversation, not to mention the rapid escape strategies they deploy to end their interactions with you ASAP. Mindfulness practices can help you become less reactive to these.

If you can give your teens the space to control most of their choices unrelated to safety and welfare, such as how they dress and other aspects of their appearance, it will serve your relationship with them well. You can let them know that you don't especially like their choices, but they are *their* choices, and you respect them as such. This helps reduce the likelihood of power struggles in more pressing areas.

Moderate your expectations.

As noted in Chapter Two, the human brain doesn't fully develop until about the age of twenty-five; therefore, your teenager's brain is very much a work in progress. It's natural to want to treat teenagers, who are so close to chronological adulthood, like they're fully capable of logical reasoning, decision-making, and impulse control. But they just aren't there yet. Adolescents operate largely from the areas of the brain responsible for emotions. Those areas in charge of rational, longer-term thinking and awareness of potential consequences are still under construction. Instead of assuming they will act and think like adults, prepare yourself for the possibility of impulsive and seemingly irrational behavior from them.

Be vigilant without becoming peremptory.

Separation-individuation includes a certain degree of secretiveness and dishonesty, and some experimentation with alcohol and other drugs is normal. Maintaining ongoing connection and dialogue with your children is vital during this phase of development. Be aware of significant changes in mood and behavior and become informed about those that correlate with problematic alcohol and other drug use, as well as mental health challenges such as depression and anxiety.

For parents in recovery, these are particularly emotionally charged issues that hit close to home, and the impulse to react strongly and rapidly is understandable. However, many changes in mood, attitude, and behavior that are normative in adolescence also correlate with potential substance abuse and mental health issues. Importantly, correlation does not equal causation. While further discussion of problematic substance use, substance abuse, and addiction are beyond the scope of this book, there are many excellent books that address this important issue.

Keep an eye out for substantial shifts in school performance and attendance, unfulfilled responsibilities, and excessive argumentativeness or moodiness. Do your teenage kids seem depressed or self-injurious? Do you see any indication of self-harming, cutting, or suicidal potential? Monitor these areas, and strive to keep an open dialogue with your teenagers about them, being mindful that anything that comes across as blaming, non-constructive criticism, or shaming will obstruct such dialogue. If your teenagers come to you with problems, ask if they just need you to listen or if they want you to respond. Potential ways to provide input include "May I give you some feedback?" "Would it be okay if I made some suggestions?" and "Would you mind if I offered some guidance?"

Keeping in mind the communication principles described in Chapter Seven and applying the skills detailed in Chapter Eight can be instrumental in helping you maintain open lines of communication with your adolescents. Although I suggest reserving intensive outside intervention for situations in which your children's health, safety, and/or welfare is at risk, when in doubt, I encourage erring on the side of seeking professional assessment and guidance.

Emphasize empathy.

Adolescence is stress-filled for both parents and teenagers. Think back to what it was like when you were a teenager, and consider that adolescence has only become more complex and challenging. Try to understand, have compassion for, and empathize with the pressures your teens face. Attempting to coalesce their identity—to figure out who the hell they are and how they fit in the world—is no small task. Ask about and express interest in their experience. If they refuse to talk about it, give them space and let them know you are there for them.

At this crucial time in their lives, among their greatest needs is for someone to appreciate what they're going through. Your teenagers don't need you to fix their problems for them. They'll figure that out for themselves. Rather, they need someone who will listen and empathize with them. Parents commonly dismiss the opinions of their teenage kids—after all, they think they know everything. Surprise them by asking for and demonstrating respect for their opinions, even when you disagree with them. Giving your adolescents the experience of feeling seen and heard strengthens the connection between you and has a mitigating influence when conflicts erupt.

Give your teenagers opportunities to earn the more adult-level privileges they seek.

Far from being entitlements, privileges such as access to a car, smartphone, or spending money should be earned by contributing to the daily functioning of the family, including chores. Connect the dots between such privileges and specific responsibilities with your teenage (and young adult) kids, so they clearly understand the link between more adult-level privileges and certain responsibilities. If they choose to opt out of this arrangement or shirk their assigned responsibilities, they also choose to relinquish the associated privileges.

The experience of having this level of choice and being able to influence part of their destiny helps build teenagers' sense of self-efficacy and deepen their understanding of the relationship between their actions and the consequences of those actions—both positive and negative. This, in turn, supports and strengthens the development of healthy wings.

Don't let off-putting attitude and oppositional behaviors push you away.

Adolescents are experts when it comes to acting in ways that irritate the hell out of their parents. Whenever we feel threatened—whether it is a threat to life and safety or simply a perceived threat that makes us feel anxious, angry, or stressed—the thinking part of our brain (the prefrontal cortex) shuts down, and the emotional, survival-oriented part of our brain in the limbic system takes over. This is one of the things that happens during an intense argument with your teenager, and it helps explain why parents can become so emotional and irrational in the midst of heated conflicts with their teenage children.

Try not to get hung up about being rebuffed or rejected when you reach out (remember how separation-individuation works), and continue to make efforts to connect with your teens. Send the message that you can tolerate their oppositional attitude and behavior and you're not going anywhere. In interactions with your teenagers, look for opportunities to express kindness, appreciation, compassion, and love: a warm smile, a hand on the shoulder, a hug with feeling, a kiss on the cheek, or a heartfelt "I love you." These small actions have inestimable value and meaning, even if your adolescents don't show it.

Remember, adolescence is temporary.

Mark Twain once said, "When I was a boy of fourteen, my father was so ignorant I could hardly stand to have the old man around. But when I got to be twenty-one, I was astonished at how much he had learned in seven years."[17] Like other difficult circumstances (and intense emotions), adolescence can feel like it'll last forever. And yet, the only permanent thing is impermanence. The challenges of adolescence may last longer than you'd like them to (perhaps much longer), but these are precious years nonetheless, and they will come to an end.

---

17 *Reader's Digest*, September 1937.

10

SCREEN MEDIA MATTERS

The art of living is more like wrestling than dancing.

Marcus Aurelius

When my daughters were young, their mother and I occasionally joked about utilizing "video Valium" (television) to keep them occupied and entertained when we had to focus our attention elsewhere or simply needed a break from the rigors of direct childcare. In the attempt to make this diversion more healthy and educational, I recorded hours of Sesame Street episodes on VHS tapes. (That was between the late 1980s and late 1990s, long before access to the Internet became mainstream and portable computer technology became ubiquitous.)

Children's healthy development requires social interaction, engagement with the real, natural world, and creative imaginative play. Yet, the immersive world of computer screens—desktop setups, laptops, tablets, and smartphones—that captivates kids at younger and younger ages is the antithesis of these developmentally essential experiences.

Screen media refers to visual electronic content created to educate, entertain, or promote and sell goods and services to users and includes *social media*—computer-based platforms that allow users to create, share, or exchange information, career interests, ideas, pictures, and videos in virtual communities and networks.

According to the American Academy of Pediatrics, children in the United States ages eight to ten use screen media of all kinds *nearly eight hours a day*, with older children and teenagers typically spending *eleven* hours a day. While this includes television, over time the amount of time spent watching TV has decreased and the amount of time spent with smartphones and tablets continues to increase. Moreover, as of 2013, one-third of all TV programming in the United States was viewed on smartphones, tablets, and computers (that number is certainly higher now). On average, children in all age groups now split their recreational screen media time among social media, video viewing, gaming, and texting. Teenagers send an average of 3,300 text messages a month, preferring texting to actual phone conversations. They spend less time talking on the phone than any age group other than senior citizens.[18]

In my earlier discussion on neuroplasticity in Chapter Three, I described how repetitive experiences create and strengthen the associated neuropathways ("neurons that fire together wire together"). Repetitive involvement with screen media alters brain structure and functioning by strengthening the neural connections that increase the likelihood of continuing and increasing screen media involvement. Increasing attachment to screen media not only distances our kids from the real world of people, it becomes an avoidance strategy to numb or keep at a distance uncomfortable emotional states, including boredom, loneliness, anxiety, sadness, and depression.

---

18 AAP Council on Communication and Media, "Children, Adolescents, and the Media," American Academy of Pediatrics, *Pediatrics*, 132, no. 5 (2013): 958–61.

A Proliferating Predicament

My intent is not to demonize children's involvement with screen media but to call attention to its realistic pitfalls. While there is cause for concern, it's important not to freak out—even though some histrionic news items describe screen media involvement among kids as a crisis of epic proportions.

Portable computer technology and the screen media to which it facilitates access put the entire Internet (along with the vast information and entertainment resources that go with it) in the palm of our hand—literally. This confers a wide variety of benefits that can help make our lives easier and more convenient. However, screen media is not harmless—especially when it takes up a mushrooming percentage of our time and energy. Parents need to be aware that their children's increasing involvement with computer screens and screen media has the potential to pose significant risks to their healthy development and well-being.

The opportunity costs of excessive screen media involvement are substantial. Time spent on social media platforms; surfing the Web; watching YouTube videos, television, or movies; or playing computer and video games takes time away from alternative physical, social, and academic activities. For many kids, starting at frighteningly young ages, involvement in screen media substitutes virtual for real-world interaction, virtual for emotional connection, and virtual for in-person relationships. Screen media provides experiences diametrically opposed to the conscious, restorative, present-centered awareness of mindfulness, using external distraction to fill a sense of internal emptiness.

Considerable scientific research confirms that exposure to excessive screen time is linked to a range of negative outcomes for children.[19][20] Each hour of screen time in early childhood is associated

---

19 D.R. Anderson, A.C. Huston, K.L. Schmitt, D.L. Linebarger, J.C. Wright, "Early childhood television viewing and adolescent behavior: the recontact study," *Monogr. Soc. Res. Child. Dev.* 66, no. 1 (2001): I–VIII, 1–147. https://www.ncbi.nlm.nih.gov/pubmed/11326591.

20 L.S. Pagani, C. Fitzpatrick, T.A. Barnett, E. Dubow, "Prospective associations between early childhood television exposure and academic, psychosocial, and physical well-being by middle childhood," *Archives of Pediatric and Adolescent Medicine* 164, no. 5 (2010): 425–431. https://www.ncbi.nlm.nih.gov/pubmed/20439793.

with decreases in subsequent time spent in physical activities and increases the likelihood of being overweight or obese.[21] [22]

Higher levels of screen time are also associated with less sleep, more attention problems, and lower academic performance and involvement.[23] [24] [25] [26] [27] Research substantiates that heavy use of screen media contributes to sleep problems for school-aged children and teenagers.[28] [29] And among infants and toddlers between six and thirty-six months of age, daily touchscreen use is associated with reduced sleep and delayed sleep onset,[30] yet more and more kids are using tablets or smartphones before they can even talk.

A Manifestation of Addiction?

Portable computer technology facilitates remarkable access to information and has become an essential 21st century learning resource for children. On the flip side of that coin, however, is that excessive screen media involvement can hinder or even precipitate a regression in children's social and emotional development. Involvement with screen media can escalate to the point where it becomes obsessive-compulsive. But while it's increasingly apparent that screen media absorption has addictive qualities, and despite the

21   Pagani, et al., "Prospective Associations."

22   S.B. Sisson, S.T. Broyles, B.L. Baker, and P.T. Katzmarzyk, "Screen Time, Physical Activity, and Overweight in U.S. Youth: National Survey of Children's Health 2003," *Journal of Adolescent Health* 47, no. 3 (2010): 309–311, https://www.ncbi.nlm.nih.gov/pubmed/20708572.

23   N. Cain and M. Gradisar, "Electronic Media Use and Sleep in School-Aged Children and Adolescents: A Review," *Sleep Medicine* 11, no. 8 (2010): 735–742, doi: 10.1016/j.sleep.2010.02.006.

24   T. Olds, K. Ridley, and J. Dollman, "Screenieboppers and Extreme Screenies: The Place of Screen Time in the Time Budgets of 10–13-Year-Old Australian Children," *Australian and New Zealand Journal of Public Health* 30, no. 2 (2006): 137-142, https://www.ncbi.nlm.nih.gov/pubmed/16681334.

25   D.A. Christakis, F.J. Zimmerman, D.L. DiGiuseppe, and C.A. McCarty, "Early Television Exposure and Subsequent Attentional Problems in Children," *Pediatrics* 113, no. 4 (2004): 708–713, https://www.ncbi.nlm.nih.gov/pubmed/15060216.

26   K. B. Mistry, C.S. Minkovitz, D.M. Strobino, and D.L. Borzekowski, "Children's Television Exposure and Behavioral and Social Outcomes at 5.5 Years: Does Timing of Exposure Matter?" *Pediatrics* 120, no. 4 (2007): 762–769, https://www.ncbi.nlm.nih.gov/pubmed/17908763.

27   H.M. Cummings and E.A. Vandewater, "Relation of Adolescent Video Game Play to Time Spent in Other Activities," *Archives of Pediatric and Adolescent Medicine* 161, no. 7 (2007): 684–689.

28   Cain and Gradisar, "Electronic Media," 735–742.

29   L. Hale, E. Emanuele and S. James, "Recent Updates in the Social and Environmental Determinants of Sleep Health," *Current Sleep Medicine Reports* 1 (2015): 212–217, doi: 10.1007/s40675-015-0023-y.

30   *Scientific Reports* 7, Article number 46104 (2017), doi:10.1038/srep46104.

emergence of treatment programs for Internet addiction and parents' growing parental fears of how it's dominating their kids' lives, researchers, behavioral health professionals, and child development experts continue to debate whether or not it should be formally classified as a form of addiction.

Addiction evolves from an unhealthy and mood-altering relationship between a person and a substance or an activity (gambling, eating, sex, etc.) that progresses to the point where using the substance or engaging in the activity interferes with daily life, becomes beyond voluntary control, and continues in spite of increasing negative consequences. Addiction is characterized by the presence of obsession, compulsion, progression, and withdrawal, all four of which are apparent with excessive screen media involvement.

Obsession involves persistent preoccupation with, thoughts about, and desire for a specific substance or activity. *Compulsion* is an irresistible impulse to act on the obsession for that substance or activity. *Progression* refers to an escalation of involvement with the substance or activity in terms of intensity, frequency, and severity. Over time, that involvement consumes a greater percentage of time, attention, and energy and leads to more serious problems in different areas of life. *Withdrawal* occurs when a person experiences mental, emotional, or physical distress or discomfort when they discontinue the substance or activity—activating the drive to resume use in order to avoid that discomfort.

Neuroscience helps us understand how substances and activities affect the brain similarly. Alcohol and other drug use activates neurons in the ventral tegmental area of the midbrain, which releases the neurotransmitter dopamine (the feel-good chemical messenger associated with attention, mood, motivation, and pleasure) into the brain's reward system, creating the experience of pleasure. Research on the brain's reward system indicates that, while substances such as cocaine, methamphetamine, and opioids deliver much larger doses of dopamine than activities such as gambling, sex, or food, a reward is a reward, regardless of whether it comes from a substance or an activity.

The anticipation and receipt of new screen media content or the completion of a video game task activates the same reward pathways and releases dopamine in the brain. The BlackBerry (the dominant smartphone before the iPhone wrested away that designation) didn't become known as the "CrackBerry" for nothing. Similarly, occasionally I hear Facebook referred to as "Facecrack."

As of yet, there is no research on the long-term effects of excessive screen media use. However, if addiction manifests as a pathological relationship with a mood altering experience that has life damaging consequences, the implications are evident. This is an area of particular concern for children and adolescents whose brains are still very much under construction. It is striking that computer technology designers and engineers, who know better than anyone how screen media and the technology that delivers it affect human behavior, tend to be tech-cautious as parents. (Steve Jobs was a famously low-tech parent.)

The *Diagnostic and Statistical Manual of Mental Disorders (DSM)* is the bible for assessing and diagnosing psychiatric and behavioral health disorders in the United States. Pathological gambling, compulsive sexual activity, and eating disorders were considered for inclusion as forms of addiction in the most recent iteration of the *DSM*. However, when *DSM-5* was released in 2013, only gambling addiction made the cut. Internet gaming disorder was listed among problems deserving of additional research and potential inclusion in a future edition of the *DSM*.

The World Health Organization (WHO) includes "gaming disorder" in the beta draft of the 11th edition of its *International Classification of Diseases (ICD-11)*, scheduled for release in 2018. The *ICD* is the international counterpart to the *DSM* and serves as a global standard for defining health conditions and diseases.

According to WHO, gaming disorder is characterized by a persistent or recurrent pattern of behavior that includes

1. impaired control over the frequency, intensity, and duration of online or offline video gaming;

2. gaming takes precedence over other life interests and daily activities and results in significant impairment in personal, family, social, educational, occupational or other important areas of functioning;

3. continuation or escalation of gaming despite negative consequences.

As proposed, although a formal diagnosis of gaming disorder generally requires this behavior pattern to be present for at least one year, in severe cases the amount of time can be shortened.[31]

Meanwhile, China and some other Asian countries already consider Internet addiction a formal disorder. According to the China Youth Internet Association, as much as 14 percent of urban youth in China—some 24 million kids—are considered Internet addicts.[32]

Appropriately, many parents worry about their kids' attachment to screen media and have observed withdrawal reactions in their children, including anxiety, anger—even temper tantrums—when access to screen devices is curtailed.

Screen Dependence

Screen dependent is a term finding favor in describing kids who have an obsessive-compulsive absorption with screen media use that results in adverse consequences, such as failing grades, family problems, emotional struggles, and in-person social challenges. In determining whether your child's use of screen media might cross the threshold from heavy recreational use to unhealthy dependence, ask yourself the following:

- How much time does your child spend engaged in screen media use unrelated to school?

- What types of screen media do they consume?

---

31   https://icd.who.int/dev11/l-m/en#/http%3a%2f%2fid.who.int%2ficd%2fentity%2f1448597234 (Accessed December 28, 2017)

32   David Mosher, "High Wired: Does Addictive Internet Use Restructure the Brain?" *Scientific American* (June 17, 2011), https://www.scientificamerican.com/article/does-addictive-internet-use-restructure-brain/.

- How does their screen media involvement affect their lives academically, socially, familialy, and in terms of their physical health (including sleep)?[33]

Recommendations

In 2013, the American Academy of Pediatrics (AAP) released revised recommendations for pediatricians to guide the parents of their patients in home management of recreational screen media.[34] Their recommendations included

- limiting all recreational screen media use to less than two hours each day;

- prohibiting all screen media use for children under the age of two;

- keeping televisions, computers, and interconnected electronic devices out of children's bedrooms;

- closely monitoring children's online use, including social media sites;

- co-viewing recreational and educational programs to promote discussion of family values concerning screen media use;

- establishing household screen controls, including rules for use of all recreational screen media, social media, and texting, along with enforcement of nightly media curfews.

The AAP has an excellent online tool you can use to create a family media plan to provide structure and balance for your kids' use of screen devices and screen media,[35] and you can customize this plan to fit the individual needs of each child, updating and

---

33 For further information and guidance on this important topic, I recommend *Breaking the Trance: A Practical Guide for Parenting the Screen-Dependent Child*, by George T. Lynn and Cynthia C. Johnson (Central Recovery Press, 2016).

34 AAP Council on Communication and Media, "Children, Adolescents, and the Media," American Academy of Pediatrics, *Pediatrics* 132, no. 5 (2013): 958–61.

35 American Academy of Pediatrics, "Family Media Plan," www.HealthyChildren.org/MediaUsePlan.

modifying it over time as your kids age. Parental media monitoring needs to be heavier during early childhood and decrease as children mature and age.[36]

Parental monitoring of children's media use, including talking with your kids about media content (active mediation) and restricting the amount or the content of media (restrictive monitoring) can mitigate the negative effects of both the amount and content of screen media use. *Active mediation* means giving your kids your opinion of media content, educating them about the purposes of various media (for example, advertising), and providing explanations and guidance. Active mediation is associated with a range of positive outcomes for children. *Restrictive monitoring* emphasizes less screen time, more time spent reading, and pro-social outcomes.

As you pick and choose which method works best for you, consider doing the following: *engage in honest discussions with your kids about screen media as well as reasons for limiting their screen access.* Mentor as well as monitor. Talk with your kids about how to use technology, the Internet, specific websites, and social media platforms responsibly. Research specific devices, programs, or apps for and with your kids. Share books, articles, videos, or programs to help them learn about technology. Above all, remember: limits can be set with love and enforced with kindness.

Make certain times and activities screen-free.

No digital devices at the table during family meals. Limit your children's screen access when visiting relatives and family friends and going to the movies, restaurants, museums, exhibits, and sporting events. This gets them out into the world in ways that encourage in-person—rather than virtual—connection, and interaction. Take your kids walking in nature and hiking in wilderness areas where the Wi-Fi signals are limited or nonexistent. This serves the healthy purposes of bringing their attention to the natural world, with its

---

36 D.A. Gentile, R.A. Reimer, A.I. Nathanson, D.A. Walsh, and J.C. Eisenmann, "Protective Effects of Parental Monitoring of Children's Media Use: A Prospective Study," *Journal of the American Medical Association Pediatrics* 168, no. 5 (2014): 479–484, doi:10.1001/jamapediatrics.2014.146.

present-centering beauty and wonders, and facilitating physical activity and exercise.

Limit access to screens in your kids' bedrooms.

This includes smartphones, computers, TVs, and video games. In-bedroom screen access is a contributing factor in sleep deprivation for many kids. Chronic sleep deprivation leads to reduced capacity in concentration, attention, and memory; has negative impacts on mood; and often leads to behavior problems.

Put screens in common areas.

Since 2010, many kids live a fair amount of their lives virtually. Having screens in your home's more public spaces will make it easier for you to monitor your kids' screen media use and mentor them with regard to it.

Role model and practice what you preach.

Screen media use is often different for parents, and you may have work-related or other legitimate reasons for using screen media. Nonetheless, what your kids observe you doing has much more influence on them than what you say to them. They pay infinitely more attention to your actions than your words. And words without works will fall flat.

Adults Are Not Excluded

According to a 2015 Pew Research Center study, roughly nine in ten American adults own a cell phone and nearly two-thirds own a smartphone.[37] These percentages have certainly increased since then. Cell phones and smartphones can be a source of both instantaneous connection and continuous distraction. It's advantageous to be able to fill time during periods of waiting—at school to pick up your kids, at the doctor's office, at the DMV—but smartphone use has begun

---

37 Lee Rainie and Kathryn Zickuhr, "Chapter 1: Always on Connectivity," Pew Research Center (August 26, 2015), http://www.pewinternet.org/2015/08/26/chapter-1-always-on-connectivity/.

to change the nature of basic human interactions, affecting family and social gatherings and altering the character of public spaces.

The Pew study also showed that 89 percent of Americans used a cell phone during their most recent social gathering, and 83 percent of smartphone owners say they rarely or never turn off their phones. Moreover, 82 percent of all adults (not just cell phone owners) say that when people use their cell phones at social gatherings, it at least occasionally interferes with conversation and the atmosphere of the gathering, with 37 percent saying it "frequently" diminishes the gathering.[38]

As a person in long-term recovery, I'm concerned about and at times taken aback by the number of people in twelve-step meetings who routinely focus on their phones, in some cases seemingly paying more attention to texting or social media scrolling than to the meeting process and members' sharing. This sometimes includes dear friends whom I love and otherwise have great respect for.

These digital stimuli sing a Siren's song, calling to us softly and sweetly, with tantalizing attention-snatching tidbits that promise enthralling if momentary distractions. We look forward to and are drawn to them. We develop a classically conditioned Pavlovian response wherein when they call we're driven to answer without even thinking. There is something incredibly seductive about text message notifications, Facebook "likes" and comments, and accumulating Facebook friends and Twitter and Instagram followers. There are so many pictures to see, videos to watch, and online games to play. There are statuses to update and comments to post, as well as emails, sports scores, and stock prices to check.

In fact, recent research indicates that the mere presence of our smartphones can consume some of our attention, thereby leaving less of it available for other pursuits. This detracts from our present-moment awareness and the ability to be skillful in the here and now. In two experiments, even when people were successful in avoiding the temptation to check their phones, the mere presence of the

---

38   Rainie and Zickuhr, "Chapter 1."

devices reduced their available cognitive capacity—their ability to think about and pay attention to other things.[39]

Another aspect of the dynamics of addiction is the avoidance of discomfort in any form. This is characterized by attempts to evade distressing thoughts, feelings, memories, physical sensations, and other internal experiences through the use of substances and/or activities. Many people unconsciously reach for their smartphones and dive into social media in reaction to stress, anxiety, restlessness, depression, boredom, or loneliness. As the American Buddhist nun Pema Chödrön explains, we become so "habituated to reaching for something to ease the edginess of the moment," that we're increasingly incapable of tolerating and being present with even the most transitory discomfort.[40]

Avoidance strategies may work for a short time, but they are doomed to fail, and when they do, the discomfort we sought to escape—whether mental, emotional, physical, spiritual, or all of the above—is intensified and extended. Once again, mindfulness practices that help us consciously observe, sit with, wade into, accept, and coexist with uncomfortable, often painful, internal and external experiences provide the path to successfully get through them.

39   Adrian F. Ward, Kristen Duke, Ayelet Gneezy, and Maarten W. Bos, "Brain Drain: The Mere Presence of One's Own Smartphone Reduces Available Cognitive Capacity," *Journal of the Association for Consumer Research* 2, no. 2 (2017): 140–154.

40   Pema Chodron, *Comfortable with Uncertainty: 108 Teachings on Cultivating Fearlessness and Compassion*, Boston: Shambhala Publications (2002).

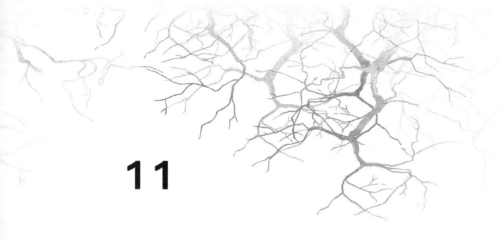

11

THE TWELVE STEPS AND MINDFUL PARENTING

The world breaks everyone and afterward many are strong at the broken places.

Ernest Hemingway, *A Farewell to Arms*

Kintsugi is the Japanese art of recognizing and celebrating beauty in broken things. Broken ceramics (bowls, cups, vases) are put back together with a special lacquer mixed with gold, silver, or platinum. Rather than trying to hide it, practitioners visibly incorporate the repair into the object's restoration, honoring and revering the damage rather than using it as an excuse to discard and replace the object. The process frequently results in something more extraordinary and precious than the original.

The process of twelve-step recovery has much in common with Kintsugi in both intent and effect. Drawing on the words of Ernest Hemingway, twelve-step recovery helps people who dedicate themselves to the process become strong in the places where they were broken. The Twelve Steps create a framework for practicing new ways of relating to thoughts and emotions; generate healthier behaviors; support the application of spiritual principles such as acceptance, tolerance, open-mindedness, perseverance, humility, and gratitude; and prompt additional opportunities for conscious contact with that which is beyond oneself—of belonging to a greater whole, of connection to others, as well as to the world. All these benefits have spillover benefits for the quality of one's parenting.

Spiritual Not Religious

Spirituality is not the same as religion. However, spirituality does not preclude religion. Spirituality for some closely connects to an organized religion and belief in a specific conception of God. For others, spirituality has absolutely nothing to do with organized religion and/or a belief in God; they draw from different belief systems to create their own version of spirituality. The twelve-step programs of recovery are, therefore, *spiritual* not *religious*. This notwithstanding, the use of the term *God* in several of the Twelve Steps puts off some people. If you fall into this group and you've been engaged in twelve-step recovery for a while, you've probably worked through this issue. If your participation is new(er) and the G-word is difficult for you, it can be helpful to think of the term "God" more as a form of shorthand to simplify understanding and communication among program members than as any sort of requirement or religious reference.

Step One

We admitted that we were powerless over our addiction, that our lives had become unmanageable.

Understanding and applying Step One is analogous to laying the foundation in the process of building a house. If the foundation isn't solid and level, it's susceptible to problems. And problems that start with the foundation frequently lead to problems with other aspects of the construction and can have serious adverse effects on the house's overall structural integrity. Moreover, if the foundation fails, everything built on top of it, no matter how beautiful and well-constructed, will also likely fail.

Step One is about finding ways to come to terms with and accept what is. Acceptance allows us to stop investing our precious time, energy, and emotion in denying and fighting against reality. As parents, we need to recognize and accept our kids for who and what they are, including the reality of their individual differences, needs, and strengths.

Importantly, the powerlessness described in this step does not mean helplessness. Step One for parents includes the need to apply the Serenity Prayer to differentiate between providing necessary structure, healthy limit setting and enforcement, and supportive guidance and giving your kids appropriate space and autonomy. The second part of Step One as it relates to parenting is understanding that attempts to change or control what we shouldn't or realistically can't about our kids creates unmanageability and suffering in our lives as well as theirs.

Step Two

We came to believe that a Power greater than ourselves could restore us to sanity.

The Second Step is about the process of coming to the realization that we don't know everything and can benefit from assistance from resources beyond ourselves. The belief that we don't or shouldn't need help—that "I got this"—is pervasive in US culture. Historically, asking for help has been associated with weakness—more so for men but for women as well. Fortunately, over the last few decades seeking help when it's needed has progressively been reframed as a sign of self-awareness and an indicator of strength. In terms of establishing a connection with a power greater than yourself, that is a strictly individual choice and the options are limitless.

Many parents cling to a restricted frame of reference and a limited and rigid skill set, even in the face of serious difficulties with their children. As a result, such difficulties usually either remain the same or get worse. A popular definition of insanity is doing the same thing over and over yet expecting the results to be different *this time*.

Step Two can restore "sanity" by helping parents open their minds and hearts to expanded knowledge and options that lead to more attuned and skillful parenting. This includes a willingness to begin to view and do things differently with your kids.

Step Three

We made a decision to turn our will and our lives over to the care of God as we understood Him.

Faith without follow-up is of limited value. The core of Step Three is to let go of the need to manipulate and control people and situations in order to get the results you desire. This necessitates relinquishing your attachment to specific outcomes. Emotional attachment to outcomes is clear whenever you really want, demand, feel entitled to, have to have, or believe you deserve a particular result.

Emotional attachment sets you up for disappointment, resentment, and anger if things don't work out the way you want. If you're attached to an outcome pertaining to your kids, you can't be fully present with them. And whenever you aren't fully present with and emotionally available to your kids, your ability to be skillful with them is compromised.

Attempts to manipulate and control take many different forms, from the indirect and subtle to the direct and aggressive. Inherent in all of them are anxiety, fear, impatience, mistrust, and stress. Giving up the need to control unlocks the door to freedom from these painful emotional states. Consider the amount of time and energy you've spent trying to control and manipulate people and situations to get what you wanted: How much extra stress and unnecessary suffering did that create for you, your family members, and others in your life?

The idea of turning your "will and life" over to anything can cause discomfort for many people. Again, the key component is really to turn over your need to control people and situations and allow events to unfold on their own—to flow with the current of the river of life rather than attempting to swim against it. You're not turning over your parental responsibility to provide structure and guidance; you're building upon Step Two's willingness to view and begin to do things differently with your kids, including bringing mindfulness practices to bear in your interactions with them.

Step Four

We made a searching and fearless moral inventory of ourselves.

Step Four is instrumental to understanding how your past influences your present, further establishing healthier ways of relating to yourself, others (notably your kids), and the world. As it relates to parenting, it's a process of reconciling your past with your present by looking at habitual patterns of thinking and acting that interfere with your capacity to be a more attuned and skillful parent.

It takes strength and courage to do a Fourth Step inventory, to identify and come to terms with the harms you caused and the damage you perpetrated during active addiction. It takes tremendous love, humility, and commitment to your kids to take an unflinchingly open and honest look at the entire history between you and consider how you've contributed to conflicts and challenges with them. Recovery helps you grow the ability to handle the truth about yourself. This process of self-examination may evoke feelings of guilt, regret, sadness, and perhaps shame. Using mindfulness practices will help you observe, tolerate, and make peace with those emotions.

The Fourth Step also involves identifying your strengths, along with the ways *others* harmed *you*. Many people find it easier to discuss the harm they perpetrated rather than the harm perpetrated upon them and their own pain and suffering. Although feelings of hurt, fear, and inadequacy are normal and natural to the experience of being harmed by others, disclosing those situations and the emotions connected to them can seem weak or even shameful. Through mindfulness practices, however, you can be present with and observe this vulnerability and allow and coexist with the emotions it brings up for you.

Step Five

We admitted to God, to ourselves, and to another human being the exact nature of our wrongs.

Steps Four and Five are basically a package deal, designed to fit together, hand-in-glove. Step Five expands upon the Fourth Step's examination of the ways in which our parenting has been insensitive, unattuned, and unskillful by bringing our conscious awareness to the specific harm it caused our kids. In this way, Steps Four and Five inform the later work of Step Eight.

Step Four uncovers distressing events we guarded carefully, sometimes for years, with the assistance of unconscious defense mechanisms and studiously avoided admitting them to ourselves, never mind anyone else. Secrets thrive and exert more influence when shrouded in psychological darkness, where they can affect us in indirect, unhealthy, and self-defeating ways. Putting emotionally painful experiences into words reduces their power. Speaking those words aloud and to another person further diminishes the grip those experiences have on us by demystifying them and making them smaller and less intimidating, bringing them into the light where we can see them clearly. The Fifth Step generates that light.

As children, many people have had the experience of going into a poorly lit attic or basement at night and being terrified by a silhouette or shadow of *something*. When they saw only the silhouette or shadow, their imagination ran wild with possibilities of what that something was or could be. But when the light of the following day revealed a pile of boxes or clothing or a coat rack with a hat on it, they learned their fears were unfounded and they had no reason to be afraid.

Through sharing the results of your inventory of wrongdoings, sufferings, liabilities, strengths, and patterns, with the right individual (usually a sponsor), most people experience a deep form of acceptance. This experience opens the door to self-acceptance—even with all your past mistakes and imperfections. And self-acceptance is requisite for healing.

Step Six

We were entirely ready to have God remove all these defects of character.

In Step Six, the two areas of focus are to identify the specific aspects of your personality that get in the way of your learning, growth, and healing and become ready to relinquish them. The Sixth Step is about becoming consciously aware of the "defects of character" that pose internal obstacles to ongoing recovery, the kind of life you want to live, and the kind of person—and parent—you want to be. The value of Step Six manifests in the sentiment expressed by His Holiness, the 14th Dalai Lama, that "Being aware of a single shortcoming within yourself is far more useful than being aware of a thousand in someone else."

Character defects are the personality traits—attributes, reactions, and attitudes—that interfere with our relationships, including our relationship with our kids, and obstruct our ability to be skillful. They tend to emerge and become more prominent in response to stress and emotional and physical pain. I believe it's more useful to view them as character challenges.

Personality traits can be thought of as enduring characteristics that sway individuals to behave in certain ways. Your personality is the constellation of the qualities that make you uniquely who you are. Your personality impacts your thoughts, emotions, motivations, attitudes, and behaviors. Everyone—whether or not they struggle with addiction or any other serious condition—has a variety of different personality traits: some are adaptive, others problematic. Even people who seem to be models of mental and emotional health display some degree of impatience, intolerance, insecurity, defensiveness, disproportionate frustration, or anger, resentment, or self-centeredness from time to time.

We are really talking about basic human qualities that become exaggerated and distorted, contributing to imbalance and creating suffering for you and those around you. Personality traits become *defective* when they influence you to react in ways that are extreme or disproportionate to the situation, causing harm to others or yourself. These reactions usually happen by reflex—unconsciously—it isn't how you intend to or want to act. Such reactions almost always make the situation, and how everyone involved feels about it, worse. Many of the harms we perpetrate on our kids track back to acting out on our character challenges.

The Sixth Step provides a mechanism to identify the specific forms that your personality challenges assume, so you can become more aware of them, exercise greater conscious choice with regard to acting on them, and begin the process of letting them go.

It's beneficial to be aware that your character defects don't indicate where you're "bad," but where you're wounded. Your own wounds frequently and unconsciously influence you to wound others. This is not an excuse; it's an explanation. As the saying goes, hurt people hurt people. This is especially relevant to how parents treat their children. And when it comes to parenting, you have to become ready to let go of your character defects in order to grow beyond your particular unhelpful patterns of thinking and acting vis-à-vis your kids.

Step Seven

We humbly asked Him to remove our shortcomings.

The work of the Seventh Step is to reduce the influence of your character challenges, so you can respond to circumstances more intentionally and skillfully.

Practicing mindfulness and specific spiritual principles modifies the problematic personality traits that obstruct progress toward becoming a healthier, more mindful, and more content person.

Letting go of these character defects or shortcomings involves identifying and consciously applying the spiritual principles that represent their opposites. Defects of character and their opposing spiritual principles cannot operate at the same time.

I have found that practicing these opposing spiritual principles is an antidote for my own character challenges. For me, the antidote for resentment is the practice of forgiveness; the antidote for attachment, avoidance, and anger, is the practice of acceptance; the antidote for intolerance is the practice of loving-kindness; the antidote for being judgmental is the practice of compassion—for myself and others; the antidote for arrogance is the practice of humility; the antidote for desire and self-pity is the practice of gratitude; and the antidote for anxiety and fear is the practice of trust and faith.

Personality structure is a stubborn phenomenon, and no matter how long or how consistently you practice, you may never fully rid yourself of your problematic personality characteristics. However, with the ongoing application of awareness and action, you can gradually sand down the sharp edges, so they no longer lacerate and draw blood. Their presence and influence will progressively fade and become less likely to emerge like automatic reflexes when you experience difficult, stressful, and painful situations. As this happens, you create less suffering for yourself and those you care about, particularly your kids.

Step Eight

We made a list of all persons we had harmed and became willing to make amends to them all.

By acting out on our character challenges, often in response to our own pain, we harmed others, including our kids. Step Eight is about acknowledging responsibility for the injuries we inflicted.

One of the most damaging effects of denial is the way it obscures our capacity to appreciate the suffering we cause others. Step Eight requires trading in this form of denial for the conscious awareness of the damage done in active addiction—to others and to yourself. It requires answers to the these questions: Whom have I hurt? In what ways did I hurt them? What caused or motivated me to hurt them?

Whether or not you intended to cause harm is irrelevant. We often hurt people incidentally through unconscious disregard for the consequences of our behavior, especially when driven by the self-centeredness and need for immediate gratification during active addiction.

As much harm as you may have caused others, as the person at the center of the storm of your active addiction, there are numerous ways in which you have also harmed yourself. Acknowledging the harm you've caused and doing what you can to repair it can be a daunting task, uncomfortable for most anyone, with or without addiction. Just thinking about listing those you've harmed and how you've hurt them can reanimate intense feelings of guilt and shame, as well as fuel new anxieties and fears about how the amends process might go. This is where mindfulness practices come in. Present-centered awareness of your thoughts and conscious contact with your emotions, without being swamped by them or running from them, facilitates the work of Step Eight.

Step Nine

We made direct amends to such people wherever possible, except when to do so would injure them or others.

The Ninth Step provides the opportunity to make restitution to those we have harmed while repairing our relationships with others. In making amends, we find the capacity to forgive ourselves and accept forgiveness from others when offered. But, if you are working Step Nine with the expectation that you will receive forgiveness from those you have harmed or that they will automatically welcome your intent to set things right, you're setting yourself up for great potential disappointment.

Step Nine is about what you give to others and, by extension, to yourself. What you give to those you have harmed includes

- your awareness that you've harmed them;

- your awareness of the specific ways you harmed them;

- taking responsibility for your actions by committing the time, attention, and energy required to make amends to them;

- repairing the damage you've done to the best of your ability through the amends you make to them.

While an apology is often part of the process of making amends, they are not the same thing—amends go beyond apologies. A basic apology consists of admitting an error or wrong and expressing regret for it. In order for apologies to be effective, they need to focus on the other person's needs and feelings, not your own. In contrast to trying to make yourself feel better or avoid the consequences of your behavior, a true apology is a tool for taking responsibility for your actions and their impacts and repairing ruptures in your relationships.

Genuine apologies need to include (1) a clear statement expressing your remorse and regret for what happened as well as (2) an empathic acknowledgment of the impact your actions had on the other person. The message of empathy is critical in order for the other person to feel as though you truly understand how your actions affected him or her, for example, "I can only imagine how hurtful (or upsetting, confusing, disappointing) my actions must have been for you." A request for forgiveness is optional. Keep in mind that no matter how heartfelt the apology, it has little meaning if the behavior that necessitated it continues.

Apologies are important, but they're not enough. Making amends involves doing everything possible to right a wrong and repair the damage you caused. This includes making changes in your attitude and behavior and doing things differently.

Anxiety and fear about the outcome of the amends process is normal and natural. After all, unless you've learned how to predict the future, there's no way to know how the process will go with any given person. Using the mindfulness practice of anchoring your awareness and attention in the present moment, and returning it to the here and now when it drifts, will help you here. As always, you can only change the things *you* do. How others react to what you do is beyond your control.

Opening up old wounds is never to be approached lightly as it can easily result in further pain and injury. In order to be recovery-supportive, the amends process needs to be done with appropriate preparation and guidance, positive intent, and conscious awareness. In the Ninth Step, older wounds are reopened only to provide an opportunity for them to heal properly.

The truth is often healing, but it can also be used as a weapon. Honesty employed mindlessly and without compassion can be hurtful and even cruel. In recovery, especially when people are less experienced, telling the truth can be used as a way to help alleviate your own guilt, but Step Nine is not about purging your conscience, effectively vomiting emotionally on someone else so you can have a cathartic experience and feel better. Your healing should not come at the expense of another.

Amends can take direct and indirect forms and be a one-time event or an ongoing, "living" process. Close and careful consultation with your sponsor is critical in deciding how best to make amends to those on your list.

Direct amends involves addressing the harm you've caused with the people, groups, or institution(s) that were injured, usually in person. They begin with admitting to the other party the harm you caused, taking responsibility for it, and apologizing. Direct amends also includes either explaining how you plan to repair the harm or make restitution for what you have done or asking the other party how you can best make restitution or reparation. And then, actually doing it.

Indirect amends are made in those circumstances where making direct amends is literally impossible or could result in further harm to the parties you have hurt or others, including yourself. In some cases, people you harmed may have died or can't be located. In other cases, bringing up the past with people you've hurt may only make the situation worse, creating more harm and adding insult to the original injury.

Continuing your process of recovery and your practice of spiritual principles is a form of indirect amends as well as an example of ongoing or *living amends.* My living amends to my daughters include being as helpful, present, emotionally available, loving, kind, compassionate, supportive, and generous as I can be.

Step Ten

We continued to take personal inventory, and when we were wrong, promptly admitted it.

Step Ten begins with a daily review and self-assessment of our actions. Through this process, as soon as we become aware that we've acted in ways that are harmful or unhelpful, we acknowledge them and take responsibility for them. Step Ten brings together the various components of awareness and action you have practiced in other Steps.

The Tenth Step inventory means examining your actions and reactions over the course of the day and identifying which were healthy and recovery-supportive and which were unhealthy and caused—or have the potential to cause—harm to you or those around you. This self-assessment functions as an early warning system, providing important information regarding when and how you may be getting off track. It gives you the chance to take corrective action before your behavior does any serious damage and creates significant suffering for you or others. Such continuous course-correction can help you maintain mental, emotional, physical, and spiritual balance as well as minimize problems in relationships with your kids, partners, friends, and coworkers.

The Tenth Step creates an ongoing present-centering opportunity to look carefully at your attitudes and behaviors in terms of whether or not they are helpful. And if you determine that

any are not, you can make a conscious decision to change them—
starting here and now.

The ultimate goal in this step is to maintain self-
awareness throughout the day and to moderate your thinking,
attitude, and behavior in the moment. Applying Step Ten is, in
general—and in specific reference to your relationship with your
kids—a lot like cleaning up after yourself as you cook a large
meal: if you clean up as you go along by wiping the counter and
washing dishes and pans, the kitchen won't be trashed and you
won't have a huge, overwhelming mess to clean up in the end. This
kind of ongoing cleanup will help you maintain an open channel of
communication with your kids and provide powerful role modeling
for them.

Step Eleven

*We sought through prayer and meditation to increase our conscious
contact with God as we understood Him, praying only for the
knowledge of His will for us and the power to carry it out.*

Step Eleven focuses on utilizing meditation and prayer as vehicles
to further your awareness of and deepen your conscious connection
with that beyond yourself, including your relationships with other
people and the world. Step Eleven is designed to help you establish
daily practices that strengthen your capacity to sustain recovery—
and an attuned relationship with your kids—through times both
smooth and rough.

Prayer and meditation are vehicles for communicating with our
higher power. They're different, though complementary, aspects of
engaging in a dialogue of sorts. You may have heard in twelve-step
meetings that prayer is a form of talking to one's higher power, while
meditation is a way of listening for the response. Meditation has been
discussed at length in previous chapters. Spiritual traditions around
the world include forms of prayer, and practitioners maintain a belief
in its healing power. Regardless of whether you use prayer based on
an established religion, the literature of twelve-step programs, or a

belief system of your own making, the act of communication with that beyond yourself is the intention.

Your process of prayer may include a formal structure or consist of straightforward communication in a conversational manner with your higher power. It can take place in solitude or in communion with others. Praying for specific outcomes is usually a setup for disappointment. Many people with time in recovery use prayer to ask for assistance in the practice of spiritual principles (for example, praying for greater open-mindedness, compassion, or humility). Others pray for the strength to get through a particular challenge or the patience to wait for the outcome of a situation and accept that outcome—whatever it may be. Still others ask for guidance in finding their best and highest purpose for the day ahead.

One way to understand your higher power's will is as actions that are consistent with the spiritual principles of acceptance, honesty, love, empathy, compassion, and humility. In contrast, "self-will" is a function of attachment to something you want or aversion to something you wish to avoid and acting under the influence of character defects (such as impatience, intolerance, a judgmental attitude, arrogance, or self-centeredness) in ways that create suffering for yourself or others, including your kids.

Step Twelve

Having had a spiritual awakening as a result of these steps, we tried to carry this message to addicts, and to practice these principles in all our affairs.

The Twelve Steps provide a pathway to a gradual and progressive awakening of the spirit. In recovery, your spirit slowly awakens to new perspectives and possibilities each time you respond differently than you have in the past.

People tend to think of spiritual awakenings as spectacular instantaneously life-altering events, as sometimes seen in movies or described in books: a flash of lightning, the voice of God, or something along those lines. There may be times when a new conscious awareness comes upon you, or suddenly you understand something in a way you didn't before. Although spiritual awakenings occasionally happen in a momentous, all-at-once sort of way, more often than not they occur subtly and incrementally over time.

Think of spiritual awakenings as growing to the point where you can see beyond the scope of your previously limited perspective—effectively "waking up" in areas where you previously were asleep or unconscious. They can be as simple as the realization that by accepting life as it unfolds rather than attaching to what you want and striving to avoid what you don't, you can experience much more contentment. They can be as profound as recognizing that all people—in fact all living things—are inextricably interconnected with one another and, therefore, deserve nothing less than compassion and empathy. They can also be as "ordinary" (though there's really nothing ordinary about it) as noticing with greater conscious clarity the sound of the wind rustling through the trees or the magnificence of a sunrise.

Every experience, no matter how mundane (think washing dishes or vacuuming), has spiritual potential. This potential is actualized when you slow down, anchor your conscious awareness in the present moment, and pay attention with intention. In fact, each time you wake up from a state of unconscious autopilot and become mindfully aware of your internal and external experience, you have an awakening of spirit. When you come to an understanding that your kids need and deserve your compassion and empathy, no matter how difficult and upsetting their attitude and behavior, it is a spiritual awakening.

Step Twelve teaches that the most effective way to keep the quality of recovery you have and continue to build on it is to share it with others, to be of service by carrying on the message of recovery to others within your twelve-step program. This emphasis on *service* is part of the bedrock of twelve-step recovery as well as a cornerstone of spiritual growth. Service is any action that contributes directly or indirectly to the welfare of others, its ethos a connection with and responsibility to something beyond oneself. Outside twelve-step recovery, people can be of service to their families, friends, neighborhoods, community organizations, and social causes.

In giving to others what has been given to us, service allows us to pay back as well as pay forward. Many people find greater meaning through being of service. This concept has been part of many spiritual traditions for centuries. In service, we discover an intriguing paradox: through the act of giving, we receive, especially in parenting, one of the ultimate forms of service.

Step Twelve asks you to practice the principles of recovery in every area of your life. The more difficult the situation, however, the more challenging it can be to do this. In the heat of stressful, emotionally charged circumstances, it can be hard to maintain an awareness that you don't have to react impulsively. Mindfulness practices can give you the flexibility to respond intentionally, so you can be more conscious and skillful, whatever the circumstances.

12

A QUESTION OF BALANCE

Success is the sum of small efforts,
repeated day in and day out.

Robert J. Collier

By expanding present-centered awareness of our internal and external experience with nonjudgmental acceptance, mindfulness practices help us move toward greater mental, emotional, physical, and spiritual balance in our lives. These four life domains represent the most essential aspects of being human, and decades of scientific research on the mind-body connection demonstrates their intimate links to one another. The more balance we can achieve and maintain within and between each of these four primary areas of life, the better for recovery, attuned and skillful parenting, and overall health and well-being. However, this balance is neither solid nor fixed; it is almost always in motion.

Parents of a certain age are well acquainted with the seesaw (aka teeter-totter), a piece of equipment once common to school yards and playgrounds. It's a simple apparatus: a long plank supported by a fulcrum in the center. Two people sit on opposite ends of the plank and take turns pushing their feet against the ground to lift their side into the air. As one side goes up, the other side goes down.

Although the two people can coordinate their efforts, sometimes the movement of the seesaw is more extreme going all the way up and down, back and forth at high speed; other times it's slower, more gradual, and softer. Intense, rapidly fluctuating movement can be exhilarating, but it also comes with a sense of being out of control along with potential threats to health and safety—someone might fall off and get hurt.

The seesaw also represents the relationship between parents and their children, a dynamic process that is always in flux, which is sometimes characterized by erratic, rapid, and intense movement and other times by that which is gentler and more measured. Mindfulness slows the movement, so the back and forth is slower and more gentle, the ups and downs milder. While there may be brief moments when the seesaw sits perfectly balanced, this never lasts long. The vast majority of the time there is some movement as the respective ends of the plank go up and down, even if only slightly or subtly.

Maintaining perfect balance, while an understandable desire, is simply not realistic. After all, how often is life perfect? Every once in a great while you may be blessed with brief experiences of perfection, but these moments are always fleeting. For me, it's like trying to hold water in my hands: I may achieve it for a few moments, but it's impossible to hold for very long. The more I try to grasp it, the more quickly it slips through my fingers. A need for perfection actually contributes to imbalance because it creates unnecessary stress, unrealistic expectations, and additional suffering.

Pain Is Inevitable; Suffering Is Optional

People generally conflate pain and suffering. This is understandable given that these distressing states usually stroll hand-in-hand. However, they are distinct and separate entities that need not occur together. Pain is inevitable in that it's simply part of being human. Some people may be more or less sensitive to it, but no one is immune. Everyone experiences various forms of mental, emotional, physical, and spiritual pain and discomfort. On the other hand, suffering is a function of the interpretations people attach to the pain, discomfort, or distress they experience. It is a reflection of imbalances in physical, mental, emotional, physical, and/or spiritual functioning. Suffering is optional insofar as it's fundamentally self-inflicted.

Whenever we believe that we shouldn't be in pain or that pain is something to be avoided at all costs, we fight against the presence of that pain and become upset, angry, or depressed by it, and in turn we experience suffering. And there is a direct correlation between the amount of effort we put into avoiding pain and the degree of suffering we experience—the harder we work to avoid pain, the greater our suffering will be.

Parents often unknowingly and unconsciously create suffering for themselves and their children through efforts to avoid discomfort that only end up extending and amplifying it. The greater someone's suffering, the more out of balance mentally, emotionally, physically, or spiritually they tend to be. Conversely, the more balance parents can create in these four areas of their lives, the more attuned, skillful, and successful their parenting is likely to be.

The mental, emotional, physical, and spiritual domains of your life are intimately interrelated. Whatever affects you emotionally will also affect you mentally, physically, and spiritually. Whatever affects you physically will affect you mentally, emotionally, and spiritually, and so forth. Sometimes the ways in which the mental, emotional, physical, and spiritual affect each other are clear and direct, and other times they are more subtle and indirect. However, anything that affects one of these areas of your life—whether it is healthy and balance enhancing (deviation-counteracting in systems language) or unhealthy and imbalancing (deviation-amplifying)—will affect all the others.

As you become consciously aware of imbalances in your life, including in your relationship with your kids, you can use that awareness to step up your practice of the mindfulness and recovery practices that can guide you back toward balance.

Cognitive Consonance

Mental or cognitive balance refers to our thoughts, our relationship to our thoughts, and our patterns of thinking—how we think about what we experience. Our thoughts and our way of thinking are based on the information we come in contact with from both external and internal sources, analyzing this information consciously and/ or unconsciously and forming interpretations and conclusions as to what it means.

But your thoughts are not who you are, merely a part of the much greater whole. The French philosopher Descartes famously stated, "I think, therefore I am." While this realization represented an important step forward in the evolution of Western philosophy, it did a disservice to our understanding of the relationship between our thoughts and who we *are* by implying a lack of separation between the two.

Our thoughts frequently take us away from present-moment awareness, dragging our attention back into the past or forward into the future. Invariably, this obstructs our ability to respond intentionally and skillfully in the present, including with our kids.

We also tend to believe in the inherent truth or accuracy of our thoughts, leading us to a variation on Descartes' revelation: "I think it; therefore it is true." A lack of conscious awareness that your thoughts are merely stories your brain automatically and continuously generates, in combination with assuming those stories are facts, creates cognitive imbalance and the suffering that accompanies it.

Simply becoming consciously aware that you are thinking is an incredibly beneficial mindfulness practice. To facilitate and reinforce this practice, simply say to yourself, "Thinking." You can further develop this detached witnessing by visualizing yourself watching your thoughts on a video screen. What are your thoughts telling you? Is what they're telling you helpful or unhelpful? Are they related to what's happening in this moment, here and now? Try to catch the stories your thoughts generate.

There are times when I realize my mind is creating seriously unhelpful tales that have nothing to do with my present-moment experience. When this happens, I tell myself something along the lines of *My head is spinning some crazy-ass stories right now.* And with that, my thinking shifts out of unconscious autopilot, and my attention returns to the here and now.

You can learn to pay conscious attention to the stories your mind creates without getting caught up in them. By observing your thoughts, without buying into or becoming attached to them, the nature of your relationship to your thoughts and your thought process will shift in ways that promote balance. Mindfulness practices will help you become increasingly consciously aware of your thoughts, so you can observe them and what they are telling you, giving you the space to detach from them as well as question and challenge them as appropriate. This process facilitates mental balance.

Emotional Equilibrium

Emotional balance involves acknowledging, accepting, and experiencing your emotions, understanding that all feelings are neither good nor bad. Emotionally balanced people let themselves feel their emotions, both pleasurable and painful.

During active addiction, many people become so accustomed to distancing themselves from their feelings through substances and avoidant behaviors that they describe not feeling anything other than numb or "bad." In recovery, people learn and practice allowing themselves to feel the full range of their emotions. This is no small challenge, as a saying in the rooms of twelve-step recovery suggests, "The good thing is that we get to feel our feelings. The bad thing is that we get to feel our feelings."

Struggling with painful, uncomfortable emotions is like being mired in quicksand. The more you fight against your experience, the harder you struggle to get free, the more stress you experience, and the more stuck you become. This is the epitome of imbalance and a prescription for suffering. Emotional balance requires making adjustments in your relationship to your feelings. It is only when you allow what is there to simply be and work with it rather than against it that distressing emotions lose their grip and begin to dissipate on their own.

Many people's relationship to their emotions oscillates between the extremes of aversion and attachment—although some people's emotional style is oriented more to either end of this continuum—avoiding their feelings as much as possible (too much separation) or being overwhelmed by their feelings (not enough separation). Emotional balance is that space between overindulging in your feelings and suppressing them, between drowning in your feelings and emotional desiccation.

Learning to be present-centered with your feelings by observing and being present with them, without reacting to them and acting out on them, is key. Remembering that feelings are not facts, and they are always temporary can enhance your ability to feel and peacefully coexist with them. The mindfulness practices related to emotional regulation and distress tolerance detailed in Chapter Six, including the N.O.A.H.S. practice, will help you move toward greater balance in this area.

Physical Fitness

Physical balance is about paying conscious attention to your overall physical health and current physical status, including being aware of the messages your body sends. You can learn how to evaluate the state of your body continually without becoming preoccupied or obsessed with it. How are you feeling physically? Are you tired, hungry, or thirsty? If you are experiencing discomfort or pain, what does that sensation feel like, where is it in your body, and how intense is it? What adjustments can you make to take care of this discomfort?

Physical balance involves exercising with some regularity, taking care of nutritional needs by eating a healthy diet and adding vitamins as indicated, avoiding toxins as much as possible, and getting enough quantity and quality of sleep.

Diet and nutrition. What we eat has a profound effect on how we feel, how we cope with stressful life events, and how well our immune system functions. A balanced diet that emphasizes proper nutrition based on vegetables, fruits, oils, and whole grains can improve our health and well-being, help protect against a variety of chronic diseases, and extend our lives. Foods high in saturated fats, like red meat and refined sugar, cause the body to produce more insulin. More insulin means less fat breakdown and a larger appetite, which contributes to overeating.

Just as surely as certain foods make us more susceptible to disease, other foods can make us feel more energized and mentally alert and keep us healthy. Some foods—rich in fiber and unprocessed—actually cleanse the digestive system, ridding the body of toxins that would otherwise end up in the bloodstream and spread throughout the body.

Be mindful of your consumption of sugar. Increasing evidence links sugar to diseases such as diabetes, hypertension, heart disease, and cancer. Until fairly recently, dietary recommendations focused on the importance of avoiding fats. Consequently, many food companies reduced fat in their products but increased sugar, and the incidence of heart disease went up, not down, as did rates of obesity and Type II diabetes in the United States.

Sleep. Sleep is as important to health and well-being as air, food, and water. By giving the brain and body the opportunity to recharge, sleep aids in the restoration of the central nervous system, conservation of energy, and information processing. Without enough sleep, we are more likely to be anxious and irritable and have difficulty concentrating and paying attention. We also become more susceptible to getting sick, and our overall quality of life is diminished. Ongoing sleep deprivation can have serious adverse health effects. In fact, going without sleep for too long can cause psychosis and even death.

The amount of sleep required varies by individual, and sleep needs change as a person ages. Recommended sleep ranges from about nine hours a day for teenagers and decreases to seven to eight hours in adulthood. Some people naturally need more sleep than do others. In middle age, sleep becomes lighter, and nighttime awakenings become more frequent and last longer. For older persons, falling asleep tends to take longer and multiple awakenings during the night are not uncommon. Napping during the day can help compensate for decreased sleep at night. Though it isn't a replacement for sleep, by facilitating physiological rest, recharging, and energy conservation, meditation is an excellent and effective complement to sleep.

Physical activity/exercise. Scientific studies show that regular physical activity benefits virtually every system in the body. Exercise helps protect and strengthen the heart and circulatory system, decreasing the risk of hypertension, stroke, heart attack, and diabetes. During exercise your body releases endorphins—neurotransmitters that naturally help to lessen anxiety and depression as well as relieve pain.

Engaging in mild to moderate exercise several times a week boosts serotonin and dopamine—the neurotransmitters positively affected by antidepressant medications.

Exercise over the long term even helps protect the brain from the effects of aging by helping to create new neurons and new neural pathways, increasing blood flow to areas that control memory, and helping to maintain overall brain volume, which naturally shrinks with age. Exercise also provides an effective and healthy way to release energy and intense emotion.

Inertia is a powerful force; the less you move, the less inclined you are to move. But the less you move, the more stiffness and discomfort you tend to have when you do move—incentivizing you to move even less. The more sedentary you are, the stiffer and weaker your body becomes and the more your physical functioning deteriorates, causing you to be more sedentary.

Physical activity and exercise break this cycle. They increase strength and enhance functional capacity. Movement is the body's lubricant. In effect, motion is lotion—internally. Even movement as simple and low-impact as stretching can make a substantial positive difference. Movement assumes even greater importance as you age because your muscles and connective tissue tend to shorten and tighten, and joints become tighter and more rigid, lessening your range of motion.

There are three major types of exercise: cardiovascular, strength training, and stretching. It's important to find and participate in whatever forms of exercise are the best fit for your individual needs and capacity.

Stretching helps keep the body—specifically muscles, ligaments, tendons, and joints—more limber and flexible. It can ease stiffness, increase range of movement, reduce stress on joints, and increase the flow of blood and nutrients throughout the body. These benefits have benefits, too, such as decreasing the risk of injury and helping to reduce overall levels of pain. Stretching is the best way to prepare your body for all other forms of exercise.

Achieving and maintaining physical balance necessitates being mindful and respectful of your current functional capacity while working to expand it. This includes being consciously aware of the need to move your body through physical activity and pushing yourself, though not too far. You can learn how to go beyond the boundaries of your comfort zone and through practice find the sweet spot between not doing enough and doing so much that you risk or sustain injury. That sweet spot is a moving target insofar as your physical status and capacity change over time, sometimes from week-to-week and day-to-day.

Spiritual Centeredness

Spiritual balance cultivates an awareness of a connection between self, others, and that beyond oneself (God, Nature, the Universe, the Divine, etc.). Whatever life brings, spiritually balanced people are able to find ways to deal with it, knowing that even though the situation may not be okay, they will be (okay). Spiritual balance helps people find meaning and purpose, even in chaotic, uncomfortable, or painful situations.

Spirituality is broader than religion. Organized religion frequently divides and separates people. In contrast, spirituality links people together, emphasizing our shared connections and humanity. Spirituality refers to the area of life concerned with matters of the spirit, those aspects of life beyond ourselves. It includes a sense of connection with others and to the world around us—an experience of being part of a greater whole.

Active addiction shrinks that world, making it smaller and smaller as life increasingly revolves around using and finding the ways and means to continue to use. Our thinking narrows, becoming explicitly transactional and outcome-focused, and our capacity to tolerate discomfort in any form collapses. Healthy spirituality aided by mindfulness practices has the opposite effects.

A central tenet of Buddhist psychology is that all things are interdependent, yet we tend to treat them as independent. This creates imbalance and causes suffering. The awareness of the interdependence of all things, along with the practice of principles and activities that connect us more deeply with ourselves, with others (including our kids), and the world facilitates spiritual balance. Such practices include meditation, prayer, gratitude, patience, forgiveness, and what are known in Buddhism as the four immeasurable qualities: loving-kindness, compassion, empathetic joy, and equanimity.

> *Loving-kindness.* Loving-kindness can be best understood as a kind friendliness. It's an emotional state and an attitude embedded in the understanding that we are all connected and rooted in a sincere desire for contentment and well-being for others as well as ourselves. Having loving-kindness for others means they needn't do anything to *earn* this emotion or attitude from us. It also means we don't engage in harmful actions toward ourselves or others, nor do we enable others, including our children, to do unhealthy or harmful things to themselves or to others.
>
> Practicing loving-kindness means making an earnest effort to see others, including those you don't care for, and even those you've never met, as friends and extend them kindness. Sometimes we give this kindness in person, though more often we extend it via conscious intention. For instance, you can bring to mind and visualize extending loving-kindness outward toward others and inward toward yourself, or silently say, "May you be content. May you be at peace." The *tiny practices* detailed in Chapter Three are also examples of loving-kindness practice.
>
> Each and every morning, my dear friend John S. extends a general message of loving-kindness on Facebook. Such social media postings can easily be perceived as superficial bullshit. But knowing the messenger as I do, I know it is heartfelt. Encountering this wonderfully generous-of-spirit sentiment always brings a smile to my spirit and reminds me how precious this practice is.
>
> *Compassion.* Compassion is the blending of an open heart and a quiet mind in the face of suffering—both of others and our own. Compassion for others means being aware of their suffering and experiencing a heart-based response to their distress.

Compassion practice involves offering understanding and kindness to others when they struggle, make mistakes, or fail. It's a spiritual experience with a contagion effect: compassion breeds more compassion.

Scientific research demonstrates that showing compassion toward a single individual facilitates compassion toward others,[41] and that compassion expands whenever we practice connecting with others through shared experience.[42] This can be as straightforward and universal as an awareness that all people sometimes struggle with emotional and physical pain.

Similar to loving-kindness, you can cultivate compassion for both yourself and others in person or indirectly through conscious intention—bringing to mind extending compassion outwardly toward others and inwardly toward yourself, perhaps saying silently, "May you be free from suffering. May you be at peace."

Empathic joy. Empathic joy means to feel joy in response to the joy, happiness, and success of others. It's the experience of being happy because someone else is happy. Empathic joy is the opposite of jealously and envy, and its practice counteracts the suffering that feelings of jealousy and envy engender. The practice of empathic joy begins with extending it outward, usually starting with those you care about (spouses, children, parents, friends). Over time and with additional practice, you can work on extending it to those with whom you have difficulty.

Equanimity. Equanimity is an evenness of mind and heart characterized by a sense of calm and composure, a state of equilibrium that allows us to be present and available, even in stressful, unpleasant, and challenging circumstances. The practice of equanimity expands the capacity to maintain present-

---

41   Paul Condon and David DeSteno, "Compassion for One Reduces Punishment for Another," *Journal of Experimental Social Psychology* 47 (2011): 698–701.

42   Piercarlo Valdesolo and David DeSteno, "Synchrony and the Social Tuning of Compassion," *Emotion* 11, no. 2 (2011): 262–266.

moment awareness and respond skillfully without becoming stuck in our thoughts or emotions.

As author and longtime Buddhist practitioner Toni Bernhard, JD, describes it, "Equanimity is greeting whatever is present in our experience with an evenness of temper, so our minds stay balanced and steady in the face of life's ups and downs."[43] Equanimity doesn't mean passive indifference or resignation to something fundamentally unacceptable or subject to influence. It means responding intentionally rather than reacting (and often overreacting) unconsciously and automatically. Equanimity is a means of not taking everything so personally. It involves acknowledging and accepting at depth the way things are, while maintaining ongoing openness to change.

As parents, we tend to be so invested in and attached to our kids' performance and whether they behave in accordance with our wishes and expectations that equanimity can be extremely hard to come by, much less maintain. Equanimity is directed inward toward ourselves, so practicing it can include internal statements, such as *It's okay if my kids are struggling right now. There are times when everyone struggles.* And, *All kids experience times of struggle.*

Another equanimity practice linked to the practice of compassion is to bring to mind the awareness that often when people, including our children, act in ways that are harmful to themselves or others, it's related to their own suffering or not knowing how to behave differently.

Gratitude. Gratitude is about feeling and expressing appreciation: for all you've received, all you have (however little it may be), and all that has not befallen you. It is the opposite of discontent, functioning as an antidote for attachment to what you may want but don't have and aversion to what you have but don't want.

---

43 Toni Bernhard, J.D., "A Practice to Help You Handle Life's Difficulties with Grace," *Psychology Today* (April 25, 2017), https://www.psychologytoday.com/blog/turning-straw-gold/201704/practice-help-you-handle-lifes-difficulties-grace.

Life guarantees us nothing, and we can take nothing for granted in this life. Every day, every breath, is a gift. Gratitude changes our perspective; it turns down the volume on the petty, day-to-day annoyances on which we sometimes focus so much of our attention—the "small stuff" situations that bring up feelings of impatience, intolerance, frustration, anger, or resentment.

Sometimes you may have to look a little harder to see them, but there are always things to be grateful for, no matter how negative or desperate a situation seems. You can learn, perhaps to your surprise, that it is possible to remain in conscious contact with gratitude in spite of feelings of anxiety, sadness, anger, depression, fear, or physical pain. The practice of gratitude is a vehicle to diffuse self-pity and self-centeredness, increase a sense of well-being, and promote mindful awareness of that beyond self—belonging to a greater whole and connection to others. Actively seeking out aspects of your children to be grateful for will enrich your connection with them.

Patience. Patience is the ability to wait without worrying or complaining. It includes allowing time to pass between what happens to you and your response (in words or actions) to what happens to you. Allowing your kids the space to experience and express their feelings without interruption is a powerful demonstration of patience.

Your ability to focus and maintain your attention where you want it and your capacity for patience often go hand in hand. When impatient, your mind tends to be agitated, and your attention becomes erratic and scattered. And when your attention is all over the place, it is harder to be patient. Consequently, building the skill of consciously directing and maintaining your attention can help you further develop your capacity to be patient.

Forgiveness. To forgive is to let go of ill will, resentments, or grudges you have toward others—people, groups, or institutions. When you hold on to resentments, you suffer more than anyone else. Holding on to resentments creates attachment to their source— giving them power over you as the intense emotions eat away at you like acid and the thoughts driving those emotions dominate your focus, stealing your precious time and attention.

Most people struggle with the idea of forgiving others whom they feel have wronged them. While it's common for forgiveness to be confused with forgetting, they're two very different things. To forgive means to consciously remember and intentionally let go. Forgiveness is a gift you give to yourself—it's more for the person doing the forgiving than the party who is forgiven. You can extend forgiveness to others whether or not they admit to their part. Keep in mind that learning and practicing self-forgiveness is as important and as valuable as forgiving others.

Through the act of forgiveness we cleanse ourselves of the pain and anger that kept us stuck in the past. As psychologist and author John Friel, PhD, puts it, forgiveness is the willingness to give up all hope for a better past.

Perfectly Good Enough

In your approach to parenting, I invite you to not allow "perfect" to be the enemy of perfectly good enough. I'm intimately familiar with the grace of messing up, including in relationship to my kids. Once in a while I've done things with my kids perfectly, but those experiences are very much the exceptions. I've done many things well, and I've made a ton of mistakes. There have been a multitude of times I knew the words but struggled to hear the music. Perfect parenting does not exist; the ability of human beings to do anything perfectly is transitory at best. Part of the mindfulness practice of self-compassion for parents is to come to terms with and accept being a "good enough" parent.

The concept of the *good enough parent* comes from D. W. Winnicott, who described the "ordinary" devoted parent as being able to establish a loving relationship with her or his children, starting in infancy, by sensing and satisfying their needs. He observed that no parent is perfectly attuned to these signs and always picks up on them accurately, but when they do it with enough consistency to facilitate their kids' healthy growth and development, their parenting is "good enough."

Good enough doesn't mean good enough to just get by or doing the minimum of what could be considered okay. Good enough parenting means providing a secure holding environment that includes physical and emotional safety and care. It means striving to identify and meet your kids' needs, and when you fall short, making adjustments and trying again. Good enough parenting requires making sacrifices, providing structure that includes setting and enforcing necessary limits, encouraging and supporting burgeoning autonomy, and building the capacity to tolerate and work through the full range of uncomfortable emotions.

Parents who are good enough know they'll make mistakes. They understand and appreciate that there will be times when they're nowhere near as attuned and skillful with their kids as they'd like to be. However, they don't ruminate on their imperfections and beat the shit out of themselves (or if they do on occasion, this doesn't last long). They practice loving-kindness, compassion, and forgiveness for themselves as well as for their kids.

Psychoanalyst and author Jennifer Kunst, PhD, suggests it takes an imperfect parent to raise a child well. Kids need to learn about life through real experiences. They need to learn to deal with disappointments and frustrations. They need to learn to respect the needs and limits of other people, including their parents. And of course, they need to learn to do things for themselves.[44]

Parents who are good enough realize that when flowers or other plants aren't growing in a healthy way, they need to focus their attention on fixing the environment in which they grow rather than on the plants themselves. They understand that the best way to help their children have a contented and successful future is to provide

---

44   Jennifer Kunst, PhD, "In Search of the 'Good Enough' Mother," *Psychology Today* (May 9, 2012), https://www.psychologytoday.com/blog/headshrinkers-guide-the-galaxy/201205/in-search-the-good-enough-mother.

an environment that nurtures the growth of healthy roots and the development of sturdy wings.

Whenever I let go of attachment to my own comfort, it's amazing how "problems" become much less problematic. With our kids, every experience of hurt is an opportunity for healing, and every argument an opportunity for working through conflict and discomfort—for us and for them.

Growing your relationship with your kids is about establishing new and different ways to be together. When you consciously engage with them, with attention and intention, you create opportunities for deep and intimate connection, even in the most mundane situations. Consciously paying attention to your intention is the skill that allows you to transform your everyday experiences with your kids into presence imbued with meaning and value.

In Verse 9, the *Tao Te Ching* explains that the only path to serenity is to do your work to the best of your current capacity then step back. Learning and practicing the material in this book will help you build the knowledge and develop the skills to expand your capacity to be the best parent you can be. Remember, as you practice these mindfulness-based skills and the awareness that underlies them, you are introducing them to your children indirectly through the process of modeling. As your own learning and skills progress, you can begin to teach them to your kids directly, if you so choose.

Like recovery from addiction, becoming an attuned and skillful parent is a never-ending undertaking. It involves coming to terms with yourself as you are while continuing to engage in practices that support ongoing learning, growth, and healing. It means developing new and healthier relationships with your thoughts and emotions, so you can recognize the stories your mind spins to give you the space to evaluate their merit, and allow yourself to feel the full range of your emotions—neither pushing away the painful nor clinging to the pleasurable—so you can get to the other side of them. It demands daily practice accepting the continuum of life on its own terms and strengthening your ability to act intentionally rather than react habitually. It is about making conscious decisions consistent with what you value most and taking action to spend your available energy and precious time in ways that accurately reflect your priorities. This is a path of wisdom guided by living mindfully in this moment with all of its exquisite imperfections.

Mindfulness practices offer a touchstone, to which you can return again and again—to shift your perspective, change the structure of your experience, and begin to have a better day whenever you make a conscious choice to do so. Is this easy? Hell no. It is possible? Absolutely.

It's a good day to practice.

RESEARCH-DOCUMENTED BENEFITS OF MINDFULNESS AND MEDITATION

- **Strengthens the Immune System**
  Mindfulness meditation boosts the immune systems of practitioners. It reduces markers of inflammation associated with decreased immune functioning, increases immune system booster cells known as CD4 cells, and increases the activity of a chromosome known as telomerase, which promotes immune system stability.

  UCLA Laboratory for Stress Assessment and Research, "New Review Suggests Meditation May Influence Immune System Activity" (January 25, 2016), http://www.uclastresslab.org/news/new-review-meditation-may-influence-immune-system/.

- **Improves the Quality and Quantity of Sleep**
  By meditating for as little as ten minutes each day before and after work, individuals experience improvements in sleep quality and sleep duration and are better able to mindfully detach themselves from racing thoughts in their heads.

  David S. Black, PhD, MPH; Gillian A. O'Reilly, BS; Richard Olmstead, PhD, et al, "Mindfulness Meditation and Improvement in Sleep Quality and Daytime Impairment Among Older Adults with Sleep Disturbances," *Journal of the American Medical Association Internal Medicine* 175, no. 4 (2015): 494–501, doi:10.1001/jamainternmed.2014.8081.

- ## Lowers Blood Pressure
  Meditation lowers both systolic blood pressure (SBP) and diastolic blood pressure (DBP) levels.

  Michael Staton, "Clemson Faculty Research Suggests Various Forms of Meditation Might Positively Affect Blood Pressure," *The Newsstand* (January 30, 2017), http://newsstand.clemson.edu/clemson-faculty-research-suggests-various-forms-of-meditation-might-positively-affect-blood-pressure/.

- ## Helps in the Treatment of Chronic Pain
  Meditation can help people face physical pain more successfully. A study using magnetic resonance imaging technology that captures longer duration brain processes (ASL MRI) showed that mindfulness meditation can dramatically reduce both the experience of pain and pain-related brain activation. Meditation expands the ability to consciously shift the perception of pain and better accept pain without obsessing over or trying to change it.

  F. Zeidan et al, "Brain Mechanisms Supporting the Modulation of Pain by Mindfulness Meditation," *Journal of Neuroscience* 31, no. 14 (April 2011): 5540–5548, doi: 10.1523/jneurosci.5791-10.2011.

  Meditative practices can also reduce the severity of pain symptoms that become magnified by individuals' thought processes.

  Brian Steiner, "Treating Chronic Pain with Meditation," *The Atlantic* (April 1, 2014), https://www.theatlantic.com/health/archive/2014/04/treating-chronic-pain-with-meditation/284182/.

- ## Reduces Fatigue and Increases Energy Levels
  By evoking the relaxation response, meditation helps to diminish fatigue caused by the stresses of work.

  C. Elder, S. Nidich, F. Moriarty and R. Nidich, "Effect of Transcendental Meditation on Employee Stress, Depression, and Burnout: A Randomized Controlled Study," *The Permanente Journal* 18, no. 1 (Winter 2014): 19–23, doi: 10.7812/TPP/13-102.

- ## Helps Alleviate Symptoms of Premenstrual Syndrome (PMS)
  Low levels of melatonin related to PMS symptoms rise during meditation practice. Meditation helps women more adequately deal with the physical symptoms of PMS. Through research and statistical analysis, one study determined a direct correlation between heightened levels of mindfulness and less severe PMS symptoms.

Haley A.C. Douglas, Winslow G. Gerrish, Sarah Bowen, Alan Marlatt, and Kathleen Lustyk, "Can Mindfulness Buffer the Relationship between Poor Menstrual Attitudes and Premenstrual Symptom Severity?" Seattle Public University, https://spu.edu/depts/spfc/happenings/documents/haleyhand%5B1%5D.pdf.

- ## Slows the Body's Aging Process
  Researchers have been able to scientifically show how meditative practices slow down the natural processes of cell division and aging.

  T.L. Jacobs, E.S. Epel, J. Lin, E.H. Blackburn, et al., "Intensive Meditation Training, Immune Cell Telomerase Activity, and Psychological Mediators," *Psychoneuroendocrinology* 36, no. 5 (June 2011): 664–81, doi: 10.1016/j.psyneuen.2010.09.010.

- ## Helps in the Treatment of Migraines
  After eight weeks of mindfulness-based stress reduction and meditation, individuals suffering from chronic migraine headaches experienced fewer migraines per month, and the migraines they did have lasted on average three fewer hours compared to a control group.

  Wake Forest Baptist Medical Center, "Meditation May Mitigate Migraine Misery," http://www.wakehealth.edu/News Releases/2014/Meditation_May_Mitigate_Migraine_Misery.htm

- ## Improves Overall Heart Health
  Meditation lowers blood pressure levels, lowers heart rate, removes toxic hormones from circulatory systems, and decreases the risk levels of the full spectrum of cardiovascular related diseases. Due to the overwhelming amount of evidence showing the heart health benefits provided by meditation, organizations such as the American Heart Association (AHA) have recommended meditation as a natural way to maintain heart health.

  Harvard Medical School, "Meditation Offers Significant Heart Benefits," Harvard Health Publishing (August 2013), http://www.health.harvard.edu/heart-health/meditation-offers-significant-heart-benefits

  http://www.tm.org/american-heart-association.

- ## Improves Management of Diabetes
  Both type 1 and type 2 diabetics can benefit from meditative practices. Meditation increases levels of self-awareness, allowing type 1 and type 2 diabetics to improve their abilities to monitor

and manage their blood sugar levels. Similarly, by evoking the relaxation response in meditation, diabetics can also reduce the body's levels of stress hormones, such as cortisol, which wreak havoc on blood glucose levels. Additionally, a substantial amount of research has shown how meditation can help prevent type 2 diabetes by increasing the secretion of insulin.

Joseph B. Nelson, MA, LP, "Meditation and the Art of Diabetes Management," Diabetes Self-Management (July 24, 2006), https://www.diabetesselfmanagement.com/managing-diabetes/emotional-health/meditation-and-the-art-of-diabetes-management/.

- Decreases Stress

Many physical, psychological, and cognitive ailments originate from problematic stress levels; meditation and mindfulness reduce those stress levels.

Madhav Goyal, MD, MPH; Sonal Singh, MD, MPH; Erica M.S. Sibinga, MD, MHS; et al., "Meditation Programs for Psychological Stress and Well-being: A Systematic Review and Meta-analysis," *Journal of the American Medical Association Internal Medicine* 174, no. 3 (2014): 357–368, doi:10.1001/jamainternmed.2013.13018.

- Improves the Ability to Process Emotions

Recent research using functional magnetic resonance imaging (fMRI) finds that meditation produces positive changes in the brain's ability to process lingering emotions even when people are not actively meditating.

Gaëlle Desbordes, et al. "Effects of Mindful-Attention and Compassion Meditation Training on Amygdala Response to Emotional Stimuli in an Ordinary, Non-Meditative State," *Frontiers in Human Neuroscience* 6 (2012): 292, doi: 10.3389/fnhum.2012.00292.

- Helps Reduce Anxiety

Meditation combats anxiety by helping individuals separate themselves from fearful thoughts and feelings and become more present-moment centered.

Georgetown University Medical Center, "Mindfulness Meditation Training Lowers Biomarkers of Stress Response in Anxiety Disorder," January 24, 2017, https://gumc.georgetown.edu/news/mindfulness-meditation-training-lowers-biomarkers-of-stress-response-in-anxiety-disorder

Elizabeth A. Hoge, Eric Bui, Sophie A. Palitz, et al., "The Effect of Mindfulness Meditation Training on Biological Acute Stress Responses in Generalized Anxiety Disorder," *Psychiatry Research* January 26, 2017, doi: 10.1016/j.psychres.2017.01.006.

- **Helps Decrease Depression**
Meditative practices not only treat depression by increasing the DOSE chemicals (dopamine, oxytocin, serotonin, and endorphins) associated with happiness but also prevent depressive relapse.

Willem Kuyken, PhD; Fiona C. Warren, PhD; Rod S. Taylor, PhD; et al., "Efficacy of Mindfulness-Based Cognitive Therapy in Prevention of Depressive Relapse," *Journal of the American Medical Association Psychiatry* 73, no. 6 (2016): 565–574, doi: 10.1001/jamapsychiatry.2016.0076.

- **Helps Relieve PTSD Symptoms**
Mindfulness and meditation can help relieve or reduce individuals' PTSD symptoms.

Anthony P. King, Stephanie R. Block, Rebecca K. Sripada, et al., "A Pilot Study of Mindfulness-Based Exposure Therapy in OEF/OIF Combat Veterans with PTSD: Altered Medial Frontal Cortex and Amygdala Responses in Social-Emotional Processing," *Frontiers in Psychiatry* 7 (2016): 154, doi: 10.3389/fpsyt.2016.00154.

- **Helps in the Treatment of Addiction and Reduces Relapse**
Mindfulness and meditation enable individuals suffering with addiction to separate themselves from addictive thoughts and emotional attachments to particular substances in a way that allows them to tolerate and negotiate alcohol and other drug cravings from a place of nonjudgmental awareness.

Sarah Bowen, PhD; Katie Witkiewitz, PhD; Seema L. Clifasefi, PhD; et al., "Relative Efficacy of Mindfulness-Based Relapse Prevention, and Treatment as Usual for Substance Use Disorders: A Randomized Clinical Trial," *Journal of the American Medical Association Psychiatry* 71, no. 5 (2014): 547–556, doi: 10.1001/jamapsychiatry.2013.4546.

- **Decreases Emotional Reactivity and Increases Resiliency**
Meditation practice reduces emotional reactivity (irritability, frustration, and anger), decreases negative thought patterns, and improves psychological resilience.

Alice G. Walton, "Meditation Helps Tame the Brain's Emotional Response, Study Finds," *Forbes* (October 4, 2016),

https://www.forbes.com/sites/alicegwalton/2016/10/04/meditation-may-help-tame-our-emotional-responses-study-finds/#3e42f23813cc.

- **Improves Self-Esteem and Feelings of Well-Being**
Meditation practice correlates with increasing levels of subjective well-being. Since overidentifying with thoughts, emotions, and behaviors causes many of the most prevalent mental health disorders in the western world, meditation naturally promotes psychological health by facilitating detachment from those thoughts and emotions. By helping individuals learn how to nonjudgmentally let go of the critical voice inside their heads, meditation helps improve self-esteem. When individuals practice loving-kindness and begin offering loving-kindness to themselves, their feelings of self-worth and levels of subjective well-being continue to improve.

Rakesh Pandey, et al., "Mindfulness, Emotion Regulation and Subjective Well-Being: An Overview of Pathways to Positive Mental Health," Banaras Hindu University (October 2011),

https://www.researchgate.net/profile/Rakesh_Pandey13/publication/231575292_Mindfulness_Emotion_regulation_and_Subjective_wellbeing_An_Overview_of_Pathways_to_Positive_Mental_Health/links/0912f506c89b6d7568000000.pdf.

- **Decreases Emotional and Binge Eating**
Mindfulness meditation practice successfully decreases binge eating and emotional eating.

S.N. Katterman, B.M. Kleinman, M.M. Hood, L.M. Nackers, J.A. Corsica, "Mindfulness Meditation as an Intervention for Binge Eating, Emotional Eating, and Weight Loss: A Systematic Review," *Eating Behavior* 15, no. 2 (2014): 197–204, doi: 10.1016/j.eatbeh.2014.01.005.

- **Improves Memory**
Meditative practices have the ability to improve the working memory system that allows us to focus, retain, and use environmental information in short amounts of time.

Michael D. Mrazek, Michael S. Franklin, Dawa Tarchin Phillips, Benjamin Baird, Jonathan W. Schooler. "Mindfulness Training Improves Working Memory Capacity and GRE Performance While Reducing Mind Wandering," *Sage Journals* 24, no. 5 (March 28, 2013): 776-781, doi: 10.1177/0956797612459659.

- **Reduces the Risk of Dementia**
Dementia involves significant decline in cognitive functions such as memory, communication skills, ability to focus, and visual perception. Meditation decreases individuals' susceptibility to

dementia and slows the progression of its symptoms in previously diagnosed patients. In a 2016 study at the University of California, Los Angeles, a team of researchers determined that meditative practices reduce older adults' risk of mild cognitive impairment.

Honor Whiteman, "Yoga, Meditation May Reduce Dementia Risk," *Medical News Today* (May 11, 2016),

http://www.medicalnewstoday.com/articles/310148.php.

• Improves Creative Thinking Skills
Certain types of meditation enhance creative thinking skills. In order to measure creativity levels, researchers examined both divergent and convergent thinking skills. Divergent thinking skills represent the ability to intuitively and flexibly develop numerous solutions to problems that have multiple correct answers; convergent thinking skills relate to the ability to logically and analytically discover a solution to problems with a single answer. Although most people assume that only divergent thinking skills are associated with creativity, it actually requires both divergent and convergent thinking skills.

A 2008 study found that practicing open awareness meditation techniques resulted in higher divergent thinking test scores and practicing concentrative meditation techniques resulted in higher convergent thinking scores, demonstrating how to use meditation practices to promote creativity in different ways.

Leiden University, "Meditation Makes You More Creative, Study Suggests." ScienceDaily. www.sciencedaily.com/releases/2014/10/141028082355.htm

• Rebuilds the Brain's Gray Matter, Mitigating the Effects of Aging
The cerebral cortex consists of white and gray matter that allows various parts of the brain to process information and communicate with one another. While the white matter helps connect various regions of the brain, the gray matter is associated with vital information processing tasks related to sensory perception, memory, emotional regulation, decision-making, and speech.

Although the size of the cerebral cortex (and the gray matter that composes it) decreases as people age, new scientific research shows how meditation can actually increase the amount of gray matter in the brain. And by increasing gray matter density, the human brain becomes more efficient at processing information, making decisions, and managing emotions. Additional research found that among meditators the only brain regions that saw reductions in grey matter density were areas that play a prominent role in stress and anxiety.

Sue McGreevey, "Eight Weeks to a Better Brain," *Harvard Gazette* (January 21, 2011),

http://news.harvard.edu/gazette/story/2011/01/eight-weeks-to-a-better-brain/.

Moreover, brain scans have found increased gray-matter density in the hippocampus, a mid-brain structure important to learning and memory, as well as in structures associated with self-awareness, compassion, and introspection. Study participant-reported reductions in stress correlated with decreased gray-matter density in the amygdala, a mid-brain structure known to play an important role in anxiety and stress.

Britta K. Holzel, James Carmody, Mark Vangel, Christina Congleston, Sita M. Yerramsetti, Tim Gard, Sara W. Lazar, "Mindfulness Practice Leads to Increases in Regional Brain Gray Matter Density," *Psychiatry Research* 191, no. 1 (January 30, 2011): 36-43, doi: http://dx.doi.org/10.1016/j.pscychresns.2010.08.006.

• Helps Manage ADD/ADHD Symptoms
Mindfulness and meditation increase the abilities to pay attention, resist distractions, and reduce impulsivity.

L. Zylowska, D.L. Ackerman, M.H. Yang, et al., "Mindfulness Meditation Training in Adults and Adolescents with ADHD: A Feasibility Study," *Journal of Attention Disorders* 11, no. 6 (May 2008): 737–46, doi: 10.1177/1087054707308502.

Mindfully ADD. "The ADHD Mindfulness Craze: It all Started with One Little Study,"

http://mindfullyadd.com/adhd-mindfulness-craze/.

- **Increases Focus and Productivity**
In addition to lower levels of stress, meditation provides individuals with enhanced ability to focus and increases their levels of productivity.

  Peter Kelley, "Mindful Multitasking: Meditation First Can Calm Stress, Aid Concentration," University of Washington News (June 13, 2012),

  http://www.washington.edu/news/2012/06/13/mindful-multitasking-meditation-first-can-calm-stress-aid-concentration/.

- **Reduces Cognitive Rigidity**
Cognitive rigidity refers to the inability to transition from one train of thought to another or take on the perspective of other individuals. In contrast, individuals who possess cognitive flexibility, or the ability to mentally shift between concepts and perspectives, adapt more easily to the situations and circumstances they face. Meditation can reduce cognitive rigidity and promote cognitive flexibility.

  Jonathan Greenberg, Keren Reiner and Nachshon Meiran, "'Mind the Trap': Mindfulness Practice Reduces Cognitive Rigidity," PLOS (May 15, 2012), doi: 10.1371/journal.pone.0036206.

- **Reduces Rumination**
Rumination refers to a pattern of negative thinking that repetitively plays over and over in your head. Meditation allows individuals to distance themselves from the persistently negative cognitions associated with rumination. By learning how to observe one's thoughts with nonjudgmental awareness, curiosity, and compassion, individuals can slow ruminative thought patterns and distance themselves from problematic thoughts.

  "Mindfulness Meditation Stops Rumination, a Danger to Mental Health," Bidushi (October 22, 2013,

  http://bidushi.com/mindfulness-meditation-stops-rumination-severe-danger-mental-health/.

- **Promotes Positive Changes in Brain Wave Frequencies**
The term *brain wave* describes the synchronized electrical activity inside the brain, and depending upon the particular situations and circumstances individuals face, different brain wave frequencies

become scientifically observable. There are five brain wave categories with corresponding types of activities: *gamma*, a hyperactivity state associated with active learning; *beta*, an alert state associated with analytical thinking and planning; *alpha*, a peaceful state associated with grounded balance; *theta*, a calm meditative state associated with higher intuition and awareness; and *delta*, a state most commonly experienced during deep sleep. While each of the five brain wave states serves particular purposes, many people spend too much time in the gamma and beta brain wave states.

Through the practice of meditation, however, individuals can naturally enter into the alpha and theta states, which promote balance, enhanced awareness, and more rational decisions. Meditation promotes calming brain wave frequency changes. Theta and alpha brain wave activity increase during meditative practices, while gamma and beta frequencies decrease.

The Norwegian University of Science and Technology (NTNU), "Brain Waves and Meditation," ScienceDaily (March 31, 2010), https://www.sciencedaily.com/releases/2010/03/100319210631.htm.

Ashley Turner. "How Meditation Changes Your Brain Frequency," MindBodyGreen, (February 5, 2014),

https://www.mindbodygreen.com/0-12491/how-meditation-changes-your-brain-frequency.html.

Printed in the USA
CPSIA information can be obtained
at www.ICGtesting.com
JSHW022325140824
68134JS00019B/1292